Life at
Walnut Tree Farm

Rufus Deakin & Titus Rowlandson

HEAD of ZEUS

Acknowledgments

We would like to thank our agent Georgina Capel and the team at Head of Zeus for taking on this book and bringing it through the development process, especially Richard Milbank for the many hours editing and (p)honing he has put in to bring *Life at Walnut Tree Farm* to publication; Heather Bowen for her page design; and Clémence Jacquinet for her work on the book's production.

We must thank Bridget Gillies at the UEA archive for guiding us through the collection of Roger's images and papers held there. Unravelling the comings and goings at the farm in the early 1970s would have been impossible without Jenny Kember (née Hind) along with recollections from Eddie Lanchester on rebuilding the ruined house. Serena Inskip, Roger's partner throughout the 1980s and a fine photographer, supplied many images relating to Cowpasture Lane and activities around the farm in that period. The expertise of Gary Rowland, Roger's friend and collaborator on *Waterlog*, gave sound advice on production. At the outset, when the book was just the spark of an idea, the encouragement of Jasmin Rowlandson and Nick Hayes set the wheels turning and into a structured proposal. Lastly, we would like to thank Robert Macfarlane for his enthusiasm throughout and for his generosity in writing a beautiful Foreword.

Contents

Roger Deakin,
Cambridge, 1965

Roger Deakin and Walnut Tree Farm

Early in this book you will find a photograph of a ceramic brick set into the living room floor of Walnut Tree Farm, bearing an inscription by the poet and potter Tony Weston. 'This house was built by my true friend,' it begins, 'His work stands up, his labours end. / By this place he will be known / To those who never know his face.' Tony's words have come uncannily true; nearly four decades on from when the brick was laid, hundreds of thousands of readers around the world feel as if they know both Roger Deakin and the timber-framed farmhouse he raised on the shifting clay of north Suffolk.

Waterlog (1999), Roger's now-classic account of swimming through Britain, published twenty years ago this year, opens during a rain-storm in the spring-fed moat that lies close to the house. In *Wildwood* (2007), his epic account of trees, woods and forest cultures around the world, Walnut Tree Farm is the fixed point to which Roger returns and from which he learns, even as he journeys out to the walnut groves of Kazakhstan and the eucalyptus stands of Australia. And in *Notes From Walnut Tree Farm* (2008), extracts from Roger's copious journals record both the labour and wonder involved in living in twelve acres of meadow, hedgerow and woodland; the night-time bark of foxes, the viper-bite of blackthorns as he cleared scrub or laid hedges, and the fallen stars of glow-worms in the long grass.

Roger 'discovered' Walnut Tree Farm as a ruin in 1969; he lived there until his too-early death in the summer of 2006. Over almost forty years, he shaped the landscape and the landscape shaped him. Despite his long tenancy at the farm, he never thought of himself as its owner in a final sense. Viewed from the deep-time perspectives of tree, water and earth, he wrote early in *Wildwood*, 'We're just passing through'. But a profound reciprocity did come to exist between place and person; each grew into the other.

This beautiful and moving book greatly deepens our knowledge of that growing-together of Roger Deakin and Walnut Tree Farm. It is the record of a remarkable person and a remarkable place. It is also, more broadly and metaphysically, about how it might be possible to live well in a landscape over time – coming to know it through hard work, through patience and attention, and through walking and wondering. Here you will find a portrait told in images and stories of both Roger and the land he lived on. None of these photographs has ever been made public before. Together, the images and the contextual history constitute an important documentary history of rural life in the late twentieth and early twenty-first centuries. Great care has been taken in the choosing and placing of the images; as you read across the book, visual rhymes and chimes begin to leap to the eye. Echoes start to sound. Time passes fast with the turning of the pages; the house rises, Roger ages, children grow old – but always the land repeats its seasonal cycles.

Importantly, the story of Walnut Tree Farm told here does not stop with Roger's death, for of course the trees did not stop growing once he had gone, and the meadows still needed cutting. The book has been co-edited and written by Roger's son, Rufus Deakin, and by Titus Rowlandson, who together with his partner Jasmin took over the Farm a year after Roger's death. The Rowlandsons, too, have grown into their own closeness with this spell-binding place, and the story of Walnut Tree Farm is theirs too — as it will, in time, become someone else's, and then someone else's again.

Robert Macfarlane
February 2019

1

REBUILDING
WALNUT TREE FARM

*I noticed a chimney rising just above
the treetops of a spinney of
ash, maple, hazel, elder, blackthorn,
ivy and bramble.*

WILDWOOD: A JOURNEY
THROUGH TREES, ROGER DEAKIN

CHAPTER I

From Queen's Gardens to Mellis Green

The landscape divides,
widens to let me through
And the leaves burst around me
In a green blur buzzing by

'DRIVING THE MORGAN', ROGER DEAKIN

I N THE LATE 1960S, THE ERA OF ANTI-VIETNAM WAR protests, the Summer of Love and the *White Album*, Roger Deakin was sharing a spacious second-floor flat in Queen's Gardens, Bayswater, in one of the grand Victorian townhouses that characterize that part of West London. Many previously affluent areas of the capital had been down at heel since the end of the war and, from the late 1950s, cheap rents in Chelsea, Kensington, Notting Hill and Bayswater had attracted members of the young bohemian crowd who would drive the pop culture of the 1960s. Roger had arrived in London in 1965 with an English degree from Cambridge and had quickly started to forge a name for himself as a copywriter in the burgeoning world of advertising, working for such major London agencies as J. Walter Thompson and Leo Burnett.

At weekends, away from his day job, Roger and some of his friends took a stall at the Portobello Road Market. Here they sold old pine furniture that they'd bought cheaply and stripped and restored lovingly in the evenings. (The woodworking skills Roger acquired in so doing would prove extremely useful to him in the future.) This was a time when the environmental movement was putting down roots, and it found fertile ground in the capital's counter-cultural scene. Books and periodicals advocating self-sufficiency and what we would now call 'sustainability', including Stewart Brand's *Whole Earth Catalogue* (later described by Roger

PREVIOUS SPREAD
Jenny and Roger's Morgan
Plus 4 Super Sports with
an Austin Champ jeep, East
Anglian expedition, late 1960s.

OPPOSITE
Walnut Tree Farm seen from
Mellis Green Common, 1920s.

Roger in the Queen's
Gardens flat, late 1960s.

OPPOSITE
Contact sheet with friends in
the Queen's Gardens flat and
Walnut Tree Farm as Roger
found it, 1969.

Driving the Morgan.

The landscape divides,
widens to let me through
And the leaves burst around
me
In a green blur buzzing by

in *Notes from Walnut Tree Farm* as 'our bible as self-builders… in the hippieish days of the 1970s'), became popular talking points. Suitably inspired, Roger and his friends began to take holidays at a remote rented cottage near Bungay in Suffolk.

Roger had been making forays into rural East Anglia since his Cambridge days and it was then that the notion of finding and restoring a ruined timber-framed house – an idea that set him on the road to Walnut Tree Farm – first took root. During the summer of 1969 Roger made a number of reconnaissance trips in a sky-blue Morgan, often accompanied by his girlfriend Jenny Hind, to find a permanent base. They always took a camera with them so they could snap promising locations for discussion later, back in town. It is here, amongst photographs of friends chatting and hanging out in Queen's Gardens, that we catch our first sight of Walnut Tree Farm: glimpsed through ash-dappled sunlight, its tired thatch and flaking plaster offer a dream of reconnection with the land, of creativity and self-sufficiency. What a prospect it must have been for the group who gathered on those late summer evenings, sipping their wine whilst pondering the promise – and the challenge – of a ruined sixteenth-century farmhouse in deepest Suffolk.

The village of Mellis, near the market town of Eye, sits on Suffolk's northern edge not far from the River Waveney, which marks the county boundary with Norfolk. The village is dispersed around a 150-acre grazing common with houses set back from the

OVERLEAF
Contact sheet detail of Walnut Tree Farm as Roger found it in 1969. Its decaying roof and earth walls were home to numerous species of birds and insects.

narrow road that runs down the middle of the common. In spring, when the trees and hedges come into leaf, many of the properties become nearly invisible from the road, causing great frustration for the numerous twenty-first-century delivery drivers navigating beyond the reach of satnav. Walnut Tree Farm is one of these, broadside on to the common. An unmade track leads you over the grass and under mature ash trees to the farm and its adjoining buildings. A large walnut tree holds much of the sky between house and barns. The brick path beneath it winds its way to the south-facing front door, which looks across an unkempt lawn to a moat whose deep waters, overhung by a coppiced hazel and skimmed by innumerable

RIGHT
Detail of Walnut Tree Farm, 1969, showing the front doors of the three farm labourers' cottages into which the house was divided in the eighteenth or nineteenth century.

OPPOSITE
Map of Walnut Tree Farm from the deeds of sale to Roger, 1970. The house and moat are in the upper part of the map, just left of centre; while Cowpasture Lane runs along the south-western edge of the property.

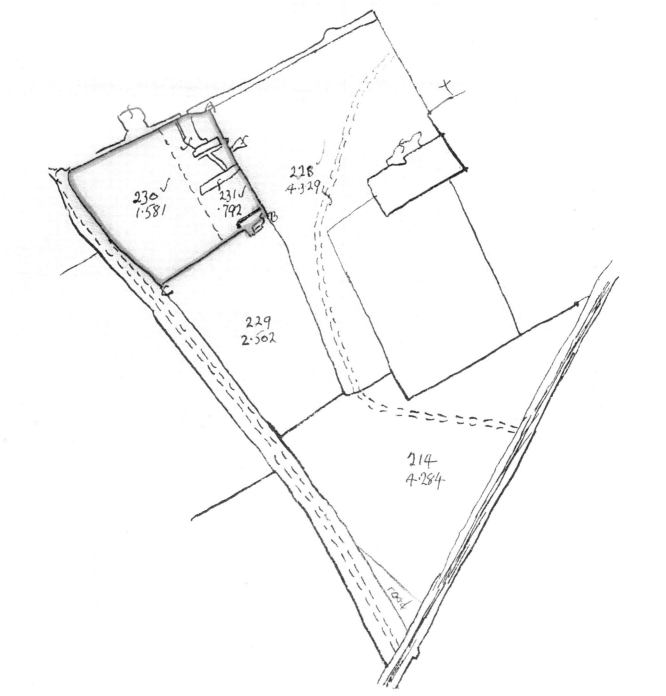

View towards Mellis
Common from the overgrown
farm garden, mature walnut
tree on left, 1969.

ABOVE LEFT
The farmhouse glimpsed through the branches of the walnut tree, 1969.

ABOVE RIGHT
The initial strip-down of walls near the central chimney stack revealed extensive rot to the principal timbers of the house frame, winter 1970–71.

dragonflies in summer, run parallel with the house itself.

The garden blends into meadow without fence or hedge. Beyond it, the four small fields that make up the farm's 12 acres are divided by a mile of hedgerow. The south-western edge runs along part of the ancient droving track of Cowpasture Lane. A quarter of a mile from the house, the lane is traversed by the rails of the London-to-Norwich main line, which forms the south-eastern border of the farm. Beyond the lane and track are the prairie-like fields of modern agriculture; faint lines in satellite images marking where hedges once divided them into fields of only a few acres.

A marker near the foot-crossing over the railway tracks shows 90 miles to central London: this part of north Suffolk and south Norfolk, served by the station at Diss some five miles away, is too far from the capital for all but the most committed commuters. Norwich is 27 miles to the north and Ipswich 22 miles to the south. The farming community that had dominated the area for centuries thinned out greatly after the Second World War as agriculture became increasingly mechanized. By the late 1960s, when Roger and friends arrived, many local properties had fallen into disrepair – either abandoned or used for keeping livestock. Such was the state of Walnut Tree Farm: a dilapidated, timber-framed farmhouse, surrounded by traditional small fields bordered by thick hedgerows. It was exactly the sort of place Roger had envisioned as an undergraduate.

OPPOSITE
The south-western end of the ground floor, winter 1970–71. When Roger first moved in, this was the most habitable part of the house.

Jenny on the moat side of the house, winter 1970–71. The rotten thatch was stripped off the roof and old tin sheets put in place as a temporary weatherproofing measure.

As summer drew to a close, plans were laid around the kitchen table, solicitors hired and documents signed. The purchase of Walnut Tree Farm was completed on 16 September. Without delay, Roger headed north up the A10 in his Austin Mini van to Cambridge (there was no M11 in those days), turned east on the A14 to Bury St Edmunds, then north-east on the A143 before negotiating the B-roads that took him at last to the vast grazing common of Mellis Green and the ruined house at its edge. There was no track leading from the road to the house in those days, and therefore no way of driving the van up to the farm on this first evening; and so, with darkness falling, Roger decided to park in the churchyard of St Mary's, Mellis. It was there that he spent his first night as owner of Walnut Tree Farm: 'slept in van in churchyard', runs his terse diary note.

He started work on the farm the next day, probably unaware as he did so of the enormity of the project he was taking on. The house had not been lived in since the mid-1950s when it had been abandoned by its farm labourer tenants because of its poor state of repair. The previous owner, Arthur Cousins of neighbouring Cowpasture Farm, had kept pigs on the ground floor and chickens upstairs. Their messy occupancy was all too evident, and Roger spent much of the first day 'shovelling shit'. That night, 17 September 1970, after he had 'moved furniture into garden', he 'slept in the house' for the first time. The problem of access needed to be addressed

16TH Sept: Drove van up to Pellis & slept in churchyard.

17TH — Scythed down nettles, brambles, wilderness, horseradish.

18TH: Scything ~~brambles~~ nettles,, clearing moat,

16TH Sept: Drove to Pellis — slept in van in churchyard.

17TH Sept: Moved furniture into garden. Shovelled shit out of end room, swept out the ceiling & walls. Slept in house

Friday
18th Sept: Patched up and washed the windows all covered in green mildew — cobwebs

Monday 21st Sept. — week.

Back up to Nellis.

Scything down the nettles, brambles, horseradish. Clearing the old chicken netting out of the garden. Clearing out the straw from the house — and burning it. Cleaning out the upstairs — straw out of windows. Shovelling solid shit off floorboards.

Tues: Mend upstairs windows Temporarily — and patch up with bits of wood and hardboard. Start killing off nettles with watering can & nettle killer.

Drove up on Saturday morning in drenching rain. Took some old pine pannelled shutters (from a truckel the night before) and made a door from one for the end room. I covered it with polystyrene and bits of cardboard to make it warmer + fit better.

Meanwhile, Jenny pulled down the partition wall across the centre of the main bedroom upstairs.

Then I started dismantling the contents of the main inglenook. First the circular brick copper then the more recent brick fireplace and grate, then the brick oven. & I got a lot of complete old bricks out of this which I cleaned and **stacked**. Inside the inglenook is vast. About 8 feet across, three feet deep, and bridged by a beam at the eye level. You could get about six people

immediately: Roger had applied for, and been granted – by the Reeve of the Common – permission for a track to be built across the common to link the house to the road. Over the autumn, many tons of rubble and aggregate would be laid to make the specified gravel road.

Soon the East Anglian winter rolled in, cold Siberian winds dumping heavy rain and snow on the leaking roof of Walnut Tree Farm. Friends came up at weekends to lend a hand and to be a part of Roger's extraordinary undertaking. The house was stripped to its bare and quite rotten Elizabethan timber frame, but a small area of tin and thatched roof was left in place at the less rotten southern end. Here they camped, by the light of candles and oil lamps. Cooking took place '…outside, Red Indian style, on an open fire in a hearth of half-bricks'.

Throughout the winter of 1970–71 plans were drawn up for the restoration of the house in a manner as faithful as possible to its sixteenth-century origins; materials were salvaged from other timber-framed houses and barns that were being demolished in the area – common practice in the 1970s, when the system of 'listing' buildings of historical value was still in its infancy. By early spring 1971 the fragile frame was held up by temporary supports, and sections that were beyond repair had been removed. Soon the long cold nights of winter would give way to warmer days – and the start of the rebuilding of Walnut Tree Farm.

OPPOSITE
Ground-floor room at the south-western end of the farm, winter 1970–71.

Roger and friend stripping
thatch from the roof and
patching it with old tin
sheets, winter 1970–71.

RIGHT
Window and crumbling earth
wall, moat side of the house,
winter 1970–71.

LIFE AT WALNUT TREE FARM

... stacking them carefully in the lorry, packing straw between each row, to prevent breakages. Thence over to Mellis, all riding in the lorry, over the Green to the house, where we unloaded in the dark with a chain — 4 tiles at a time (20 lbs a go).

<u>Sunday</u> we pulled down the ceiling in the end room. Finished making a way through (breaking down the brick wall). and repaired holes in the thatch roof with corrugated iron. Also pulled out all the wet thatch and ~~stuff~~ damp clay from round. The upstairs plate which showed signs of fungal decay. Cleared out rubble, and knocked down partition wall upstairs.

The moat looking south-west
towards Cowpasture Lane,
winter 1970–71.

CHAPTER 2

The House that Roger Rebuilt

Only with a great deal of work, and love,
can you truly take possession of a house.

'THE HOUSE', CHAPTER NOTES

B Y LATE 1970 THE DETERIORATING WEATHER
and the size of the task in hand had forced Roger and
his friends to beat a retreat to the warmth and shelter of
Queen's Gardens. They were not in any way disheartened,
but they had reached a more realistic view of the project they had
taken on: rebuilding a 500-year-old farmhouse was going to be a
rather more demanding activity than stripping old furniture and
rubbing beeswax into the grain.

That winter, Roger contacted local Suffolk builders and held
meetings at the farm. Building firms in the area were familiar with
working on traditional timber-framed structures, since a large proportion of the housing stock in the area dated back to the seven-
teenth century and earlier. The development booms in the decades
following Roger's purchase of the farm, and the frequent demolition
of old buildings in the 1960s and 1970s, had seen that proportion
fall significantly, but many still remain, disguised behind later brick
facades. The builders who met Roger at Walnut Tree Farm may well
have thought that the best approach to this mouldering structure
would be to douse it in paraffin, light a Swan Vesta and stand well
back. But Roger was set not on pyrotechnics but on igniting the
enthusiasm of others for the task of rebuilding the place. As well
as evaluating and comparing the various estimates he received
(like anyone having their house redecorated), he had to make sure
the chosen builder was open to the idea of working closely with

PREVIOUS SPREAD
Walnut Tree Farm on a winter
morning, 1973–74.

OPPOSITE
Strip-down and repair in
full swing, spring 1971. The
rafters at the farm's north-
eastern end were beyond
saving, but its opposite end
was still habitable.

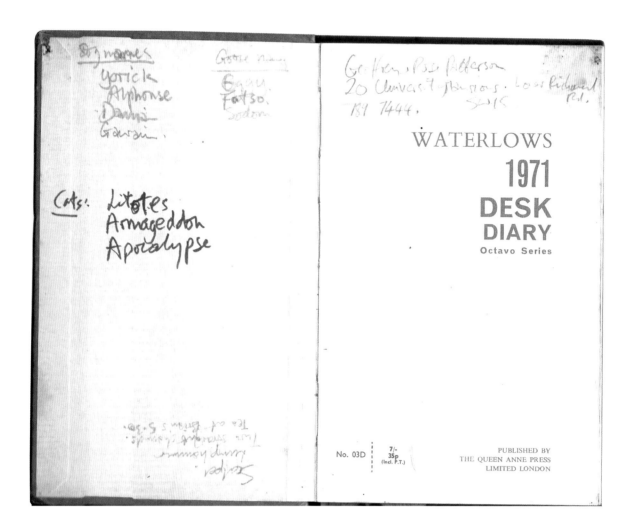

Dog names
Yorick
Alphonse
Dennis
Gawain.

Goose name
Esau
Fat 30.
Sodom.

Cats: Litotes
Armageddon
Apocalypse

Geoffrey, Rose Patterson
20 Univers... houses, ... Richard Rd.
181 7444.   ...15

WATERLOWS
1971
DESK
DIARY
Octavo Series

No. 03D | 7/-
          35p
       (Incl. P.T.)

PUBLISHED BY
THE QUEEN ANNE PRESS
LIMITED LONDON

April 1971

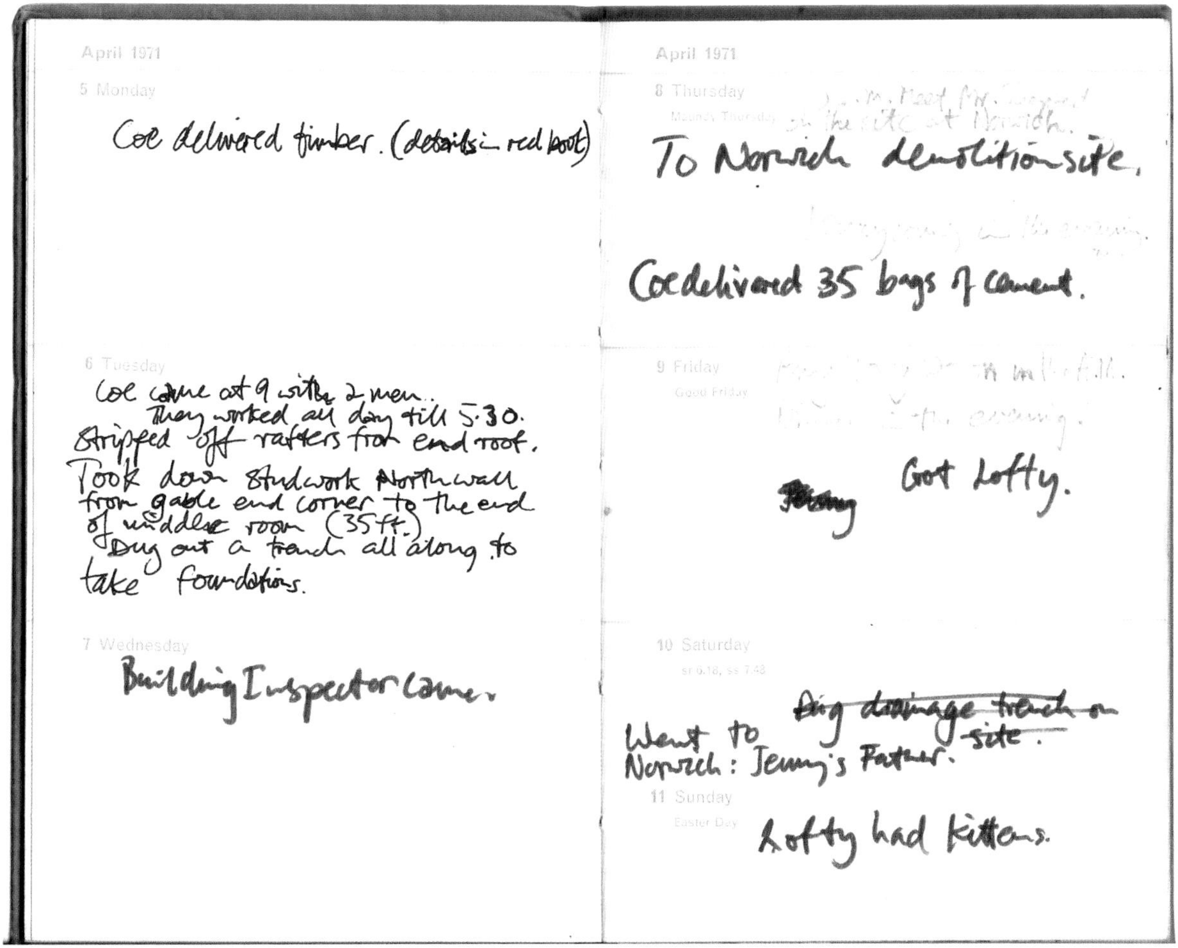

5 Monday

Coe delivered timber. (details in red book)

6 Tuesday

Coe came at 9 with 2 men.
They worked all day till 5.30.
Stripped off rafters from end roof.
Took down studwork North wall
from gable end corner to the end
of middle room (35 ft.)
Dug out a trench all along to
take foundations.

7 Wednesday

Building Inspector came.

April 1971

8 Thursday
Maundy Thursday

To Norwich demolition site.

Coe delivered 35 bags of cement.

9 Friday
Good Friday

~~Fixing~~ Got Lofty.

10 Saturday
sr 6.18, ss 7.48

~~Dig drainage trench on site.~~
Went to Norwich: Jenny's Father.

11 Sunday
Easter Day

Lofty had kittens.

THE HOUSE THAT ROGER REBUILT

him and his friends. Roger was as keen as ever to take a literally 'hands on' approach to the rebuilding of Walnut Tree Farm, but he was aware that certain aspects of the work – notably roofing, electrical wiring and rebuilding the brick chimney stacks – would need to be handled by seasoned professionals. His diary entry for Sunday 28 February, 1971 reads: 'Saw Mr. Coe and Mr. Wright, will decide next week who's to build.' By early March Roger had decided that Mr Coe – recommended by an architect friend and based in Redlingfield, just half a dozen miles or so from Mellis – was the man for the job. Accompanied by his trade companions, he was to start work in a month or so, when the spring days would be longer and drier. In the meantime, basic utilities were connected. 'Electricity on!' reads the diary entry for 2 February, followed by 'Telephone being fixed' on the 13th. The previous occupants of the farm, the last of whom had moved out in 1958, had not enjoyed such basic amenities as running water, electricity and connection to the telephone network. (Walnut Tree Farm was far from unique in this respect. A row of houses near the centre of Mellis is known locally as 'millionaires' row' as it was the first to be connected to the national grid in the late 1950s.)

Mr Coe arrived on 6 April with two co-workers and started stripping off more rotten timbers from the roof ('Coe came at 9 with 2 men. They worked all day until 5.30'). Trenches for footings and drainage were dug, and materials delivered or salvaged from

10 Monday

Merry & Ted arrived. 11·45.

Fitted new sill plate.
(& bedded in 2ⁿᵈ section & fitted
DPC along to end corner of
South side). 11hrs. 10½.

11 Tuesday

We jacked up the plate
next to the chimney, supported
chimney beam, and put in a
new post morticed & tenoned to
take chimney beam, & lift top
plate level with end of house.
Ted fitted window frame at end.
16hrs

12 Wednesday

We studded up the
South wall and lifted
top plate into position.
Began on window frames
and replacement studding.
16hrs

May 1971

13 Thursday

Fitted angle irons and iron
straps. Jacked up section
of sill at kitchen end of
wall and inserted DPC
to inside the kitchen. Put in
tie rod & tightened the house. 16hrs.
Put up 1ˢᵗ collar and putting 2 rafters
A → next to chimney,
and pulled in gable end,
with scaffold pole & arrow
jack to level. LORRY DELIVERED
TIMBER.
Fri: Put up other purlin & tied
them to section of roof other side
of chimney. Put in a ridge board
and put up rafters.
16hrs:

14 Friday

TOTAL HOURS: 8½hrs

15 Saturday

Whitsunday—Scottish Quarter Day sr 5.10, ss 8.45

16 Sunday

5th after Easter Rogation Sunday

11a.m. Mr. Howlett.

OPPOSITE
Roger's day-to-day-diary
of the rebuild, May 1971.

LEFT
Roger repairing the
south-eastern end of the
roof, summer 1971.

Sketches for the northwestern gable end and lean-to floor plan, 1971.

LIFE AT WALNUT TREE FARM

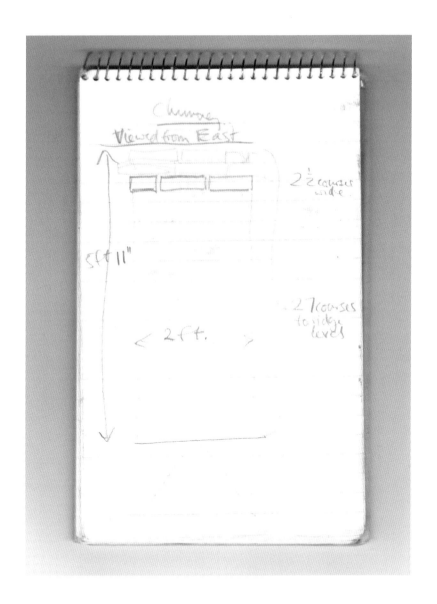

Chimney repair sketch plan, 1971 (see page 43).

other ruined houses. Alongside Roger, his London friends Bullus Hutton, Dudley Young, Jenny Hind, Tony Axon, Tony Weston and others, local folk were enlisted to help, many of them becoming friends of Roger's and participating in projects at the farm. Looking through one diary from 1971 the names of Brian, Eddie, Peter, Ginger, Mervyn and Ted feature more and more as the weeks go by and Mr Coe's contributions to the work clearly begin to wane. As Roger started to make connections in Suffolk, he gradually gained the confidence to complete the rebuild of the farm under his own direction. Sometimes Brian, Eddie and Roger worked long days together, sometimes just a few hours in the evening.

RIGHT
Roger chats to local children, with Brian McGuinness looking on, summer 1971.

OPPOSITE
Stripping and repairing the south-eastern end of the house, summer 1971. The back door of the end cottage, facing the moat, would become Roger's front door.

A view of the area that would become the kitchen of the rebuilt Walnut Tree Farm, summer 1971. At that time the central fireplace, visible in the background (along with Roger himself), was used as a temporary kitchen and living room.

The rebuild continues,
mid-May 1971.

May 1971

17 Monday

9a.m. Mervyn & Ted: 1) Put in trimmer across
chimney; fitted 4 old rafters to it
on south side by chimney.
2) Framed in new
dormer on South side of house.
(Took all afternoon.) 3) Sanded down South side
studwork, sledged off replacement rafters for
North Side (2 of them).

/   16 hrs

18 Tuesday   Send off Coe's cheque.
Dean's cheque.

Margot. 7.33 train.
Mervyn + Ted — 8 hrs. each. = 16 } 23 hrs
Two more Chippies. 3½ hrs each. = 7 }
Morning: Finished off end dormer. Wound up
angle bracket. Put in middle tie rod
P.M: Framed in 2 dormers (4 chippies).
— Began on them, anyway.
I sanded off chimney trimmers & Protimed

19 Wednesday   Arrived at 9
Mervyn & Ted all day (Left at 5).
Finished off both dormers. Repaired
The two faulty rafters (by putting in a
trimmer level with the window trimmer).
Took down ceiling joists, denailed the
Protimed wood.
Tony + Margot here.   Began jacking up the
Gable.   Removed thatch
Saw Eddie. Must order Battens, fibreglass
& leading.   16 hrs

58

20 Thursday
Ascension Day

Marvyn + Ted. Fixed ceiling joists
and Chimney trimmers.
Did new roof section of springers.
Tony + I collected 180 ft. of 5/8"
matchboarding from Clark's.
Sanded off rafters ready for boarding.

16 hrs.

21 Friday

M + T did the flue spars and
the springers, all along N. side
also fixed matchboarding.
I sanded off all rafters on N side 16 hrs
+ protuned them. Tony dug
trench in ditch + cleared rubble
from fireplace.

Total : 87 hours   Last 2 weeks should
cost £137.76.

22 Saturday
sr 5.0, ss 8.0

Tony drained + piped the ditch
3 Americans dug out rest of
centre floor + barrowed away. Took out
end floorboards. Dug out under gable
end. Took out centre room partitions.

23 Sunday
Sunday after Ascension

Brian came and did
Ring Mr. Shepherd. gable end wall bricking.
Mr. Howlett. (T.B. + I concreted).
5 p.m. Brian McGuiness. Paid him £5.

ABOVE
Sleeping outside, weather permitting, summer 1971.

ABOVE RIGHT
Kitchen and living room, summer 1971.

RIGHT
One of numerous cats living at Walnut Tree Farm in the early 1970s. The last descendants of this original generation are still holding out around the farm.

ABOVE
Roger's Morgan Plus 4 Super
Sports taken from inside the
house – looking towards the
common – with temporary
supports holding up the
frame, summer 1971.

LEFT
The Morgan negotiates
the newly laid track
across the common, taken
from the stripped-out first
floor, summer 1971.

The new roof going on fast,
summer 1971; Jenny is in
the foreground, surrounded
by geese.

Roger leaning against the
repaired south wall, late
summer 1971. Windows
and walls being fixed before
the weather turns.

His diary for the week beginning 17 May shows that on four days as much as sixteen hours' work was carried out. Diary entries reading 'No Brian' indicated no-shows. Brian had the reputation of being a Suffolk Wildman, rumoured to be proficient in the ways of poaching and hare coursing, amongst other activities.

Over the summer months work proceeded intensively, with little let-up. The house was opened up from the three cramped farm labourers' cottages into which it had been divided, probably in Georgian or Victorian times. It was returned to a more original layout, with the central chimney stack and 8 feet by 3 feet inglenook fireplace serving the living room, the hearth large enough for two

LEFT
'Cosy-Wrap' insulation going on, late summer 1971.

OVERLEAF
Diary entries record Brian's work on the roof in September 1971, and a deterioration in the weather later in the autumn.

20 Monday

21 Tuesday

22 Wednesday

Tony Aaron. came & Brian smashed his van and came to mend it in the morning, so not much work done. Fixed noggins both sides of dormers. Fixed gable soffits. Brian came from 7-8 and we fixed the gable bargeb'ds.

23 Thursday

Painted gable bargeboards. Put in last main ceiling joist and felted & battened roof up to level with top of dormer on south side. Brian came for 1½hrs. & felted & battened. Cleared up the top floor.

24 Friday

A.M. Felted & battened almost to top of S. roof.
P.M. Tony Weston came & we felted & battened up to level with dormer + dormer itself on N. side.
Brian came for an hour P.M. and felted & battened S. dormer.   (B. - 1hr.)

25 Saturday   Brian felted & battened
sr 6.50 ss 6.54   rest of roof A.M.
P.M. B. leaded N. dormer and we tiled up most of N. roof with Dudley. (B = 8.30 -1.00 and 2.00 till 6.30).
= 9 hrs.

26 Sunday
16th after Trinity   Brian 9.a.m. till 1.00. 2.00 till 7.00
= 9 hrs.   39 TOTAL
(B. ridged all along roof, gave me 9 ridge tiles) we tiled all up south roof except dormer.

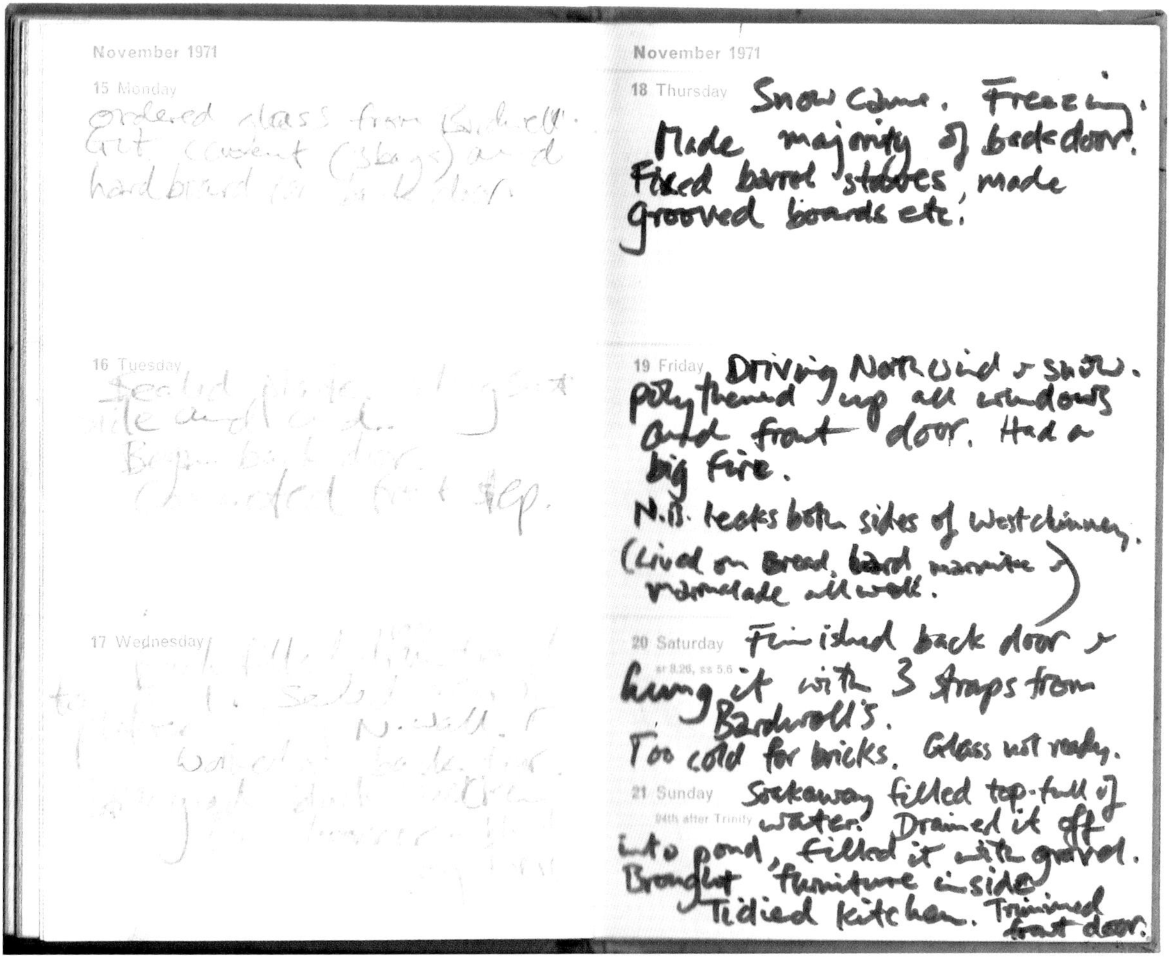

November 1971

15 Monday

ordered glass from Bardwell's. Got cement (3 bags) and hardboard for back door.

16 Tuesday

Began back door. Cemented front step.

17 Wednesday

November 1971

18 Thursday

Snow came. Freezing. Made majority of back door. Fixed barrel staves, made grooved boards etc.

19 Friday

Driving North wind & snow. Polythened up all windows and front door. Had a big fire.
N.B. leaks both sides of West chimney.
(Lived on bread, lard, marmite & marmalade all week.)

20 Saturday

sr 8.26, ss 5.6

Finished back door & hung it with 3 straps from Bardwell's.
Too cold for bricks. Glass not ready.

21 Sunday

24th after Trinity

Soakaway filled top-full of water. Drained it off into pond, filled it with gravel.
Brought furniture inside.
Tidied kitchen. Trimmed front door.

When the weather did not
allow him to sleep outside,
Roger perched a 'bedroom'
on the first-floor joists above
the makeshift kitchen-in-the-
fireplace, late summer 1971.

Roger fixing the last sections
of 'Cosy-Wrap', autumn 1971.

people to be able to stand on either side of the fire and look up to the sky through the chimney top 24 feet above. Two more chimney flues (adjoining the original) had been added after the house was built: one of them in the first, seventeenth-century extension to the original frame of the house to the north; the other in the eighteenth century at first-floor level, piggybacking on the original sixteenth-century stack. Roger had no plans for central heating, the house would be heated by wood, either in a burner or open fire with the oil-fired AGA warming the kitchen (as it still does).

Days were spent replacing rotten timbers or cleaning up those originals that remained sound. Three dormer windows were added to the south side and, on the roof, East Anglian pantiles replaced the thatch and tin. Stormproof windows were purchased and modern insulation* fitted to keep out the hard Suffolk winter that they had experienced only a few months before. By the end of September, the roof was watertight. Roofing felt, battens and tiles went on fast once the frame was sound. Barge and facia boards were nailed in position and trimmed in situ. The next step was to put the windows in place and cover the walls before the weather turned. Roger and Brian battened, boarded, lathed and rendered the whole exterior of the house in a couple of weeks in late October. They got all the windows in soon after, only for wintry weather to set in before they

* Modern for the 1970s, that is.

could do the glazing. Roger's diary for 18 November reads: 'Snow came. Freezing…'; and the next day's entry continues in similar vein: 'Driving North wind & snow. Polythened up all windows and front door. Had a big fire…' But just a week or so later the glass was fitted, the making up of the end door and trimming of the front door was finished, the guttering had been put up – with drains running to the front and side ditches – and final touches had been made to the roof and dormers.

By the end of 1971 the roof, walls and windows had been made secure, and the house was capable of providing warmth and protection from the elements. Its internal structure was sound enough for basic living. Over the course of 1972 and 1973 individual rooms would be slowly transformed from building sites into the constituents of a home. They would never be *totally* finished, though. Even today, pieces of bare plasterboard are still waiting for the plasterer's trowel.

By the mid-1970s, the house that Roger had rebuilt was ready for full-time occupation.

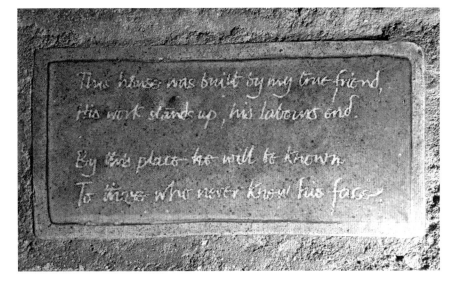

ABOVE LEFT
North end fireplace, autumn 1971.

ABOVE RIGHT
The Fordson – here safely parked on the lawn – once did violence to the kitchen wall (see page 82).

LEFT
Floor brick in the living room. 'This house was built by my true friend, his work stands up, his labours end. By this place he will be known to those who never know his face.'
Tony Weston

2

LIVING AT
WALNUT TREE FARM

*... I have ended up on terms of the greatest
intimacy with all the beams, posts and
pegged joints in the place.*

WILDWOOD

CHAPTER 3

Four Fields

The jungled hedges that surround my
four meadows comprise a necessary rampart
to the winds that cut across the open
wheat prairies beyond.

WILDWOOD

PUTTING ALL OF YOURSELF — AND ALL OF YOUR resources (physical, mental and material) – into a project that takes years to complete is an experience that is as intense and as draining as it is joyful and uplifting. The rebuilding of Walnut Tree Farm was just such a project. It created a remarkable connectedness between Roger and the place he had restored – a bond whose depth and intimacy is difficult to put into words but which could be seen and felt by those around him. After the reconstruction of the house was complete, Walnut Tree Farm and Roger Deakin were in many ways one.

The elemental nature of the farm would find expression in the milestones of Roger's creative career. The BBC radio documentaries *The House* and *The Garden*, and above all the books *Waterlog*, *Wildwood* and *Notes from Walnut Tree Farm* (the last two of which were published posthumously) continue to inspire many people around the world.

This chapter and the two that follow it explore those aspects of Walnut Tree Farm that connect house, landscape and Roger: the immediate surroundings of the farm as both agricultural environment and natural habitat; wood in its many forms and uses – from the functional to the artistic; and, of course, the moat.

*

PREVIOUS SPREAD
Ferguson tractor, vegetable patch, woodshed and house, summer, early 2000s.

OPPOSITE
The versatility of the Morgan: bringing back supplies of hay before the farm produced its first harvest for its new occupants, winter 1971–72.

Harvesting hay at Walnut
Tree Farm, late 1970s.

By the mid-1970s Roger had not only rebuilt Walnut Tree Farm, he had also found a job teaching English and Drama at the grammar school in nearby Diss. It was time for him to move into the second phase of his plan for the site: sustainable farming and nature conservation. At the time, these movements were still in their infancy, but realization of the radical ideas that underpinned them was already leading to conflict and confrontation at both local and national level, as Roger himself was shortly to find out.

Livestock – in the shape of goats, sheep, chickens, geese and donkeys – soon arrived at the farm, together with the implements needed to work the land. These were to be attached to the Fordson

RIGHT
A train on the London-to-Norwich line thunders past railway line field, late 1970s. A wood of hornbeam, ash and oak would later be planted in part of this field.

Major tractor that had been used to transport materials while the house was being restored. (Part way through the rebuilding, this same tractor had almost demolished the house when the man at the wheel lost control and smashed through the kitchen wall, luckily missing the principal beams and only dusting the terrified driver with plaster.)

The farm implements purchased by Roger – at farm sales or the weekly livestock and general auction in Diss – included a nine-tine harrow, two Ransome Robin ploughs, two Bamford Wuffler hay-turners, a mower and various two- and four-wheeled farm trailers. The tractor and farm machinery may look vintage in the

Outside the goat shed: 'Billy The Kid' cadges a ride on a sheep.

LIFE AT WALNUT TREE FARM

The farm was home to a variety of livestock from Roger's earliest days there until the mid-1980s, when work commitments dictated a downscaling of his farming activities.

Friends visiting the farm, early 1970s.

Friends' children and a farm cat enjoy a tractor ride, early 1970s.

photographs that accompany this chapter, but in the mid-1970s they were second-hand items that were only twenty years old or less. Using such machinery then was the equivalent of using 1990s machinery now. Before Roger acquired them from Arthur Cousins at Cowpasture Farm, the four fields had been worked traditionally to serve the small dairy herd there. Now that he had livestock of his own to rear, it was only natural for Roger to farm the fields in time-honoured fashion, through managed grazing and haymaking. He continued to do so until the early 1980s, when the round-the-clock needs of livestock had to take second place to the increasing demands of Roger's journalism, film-making and career in the environmental movement. Slowly and sadly, the various agricultural machines were pensioned off. The hay mower, turners and trailers were parked at the field edge and were soon consumed by brambles and thorn bushes. Roger came to an arrangement with a local cattle farmer – Michael Wicks of Hall Farm, on the opposite side of the common – that he would take the hay for his herd. This arrangement would outlive both men.

One of the things that first drew Roger to this corner of Suffolk was its feeling of remoteness, of being slightly cut off (while still being only ninety minutes on the train from London Liverpool Street). A quiet and idiosyncratic region whose low-lying agricultural landscape bulges into the North Sea, East Anglia seemed to belong to an earlier and stranger England. After the war, it lagged

Roger mans a stall at the first
Huntingfield Fair, 1980.

Haymaking on Mellis
Green, 1970s.

LIFE AT WALNUT TREE FARM

behind much of Britain in the adoption of new farming techniques. In Suffolk, certain tasks that had become mechanized elsewhere in the country continued to be carried out manually. A photograph taken from the farm across Mellis Common at haymaking time around 1975 shows a jacketed individual, abetted by a companion sporting more conventional workclothes, tossing sheaves onto a hay waggon with a pitchfork. Replace the tractor with a horse and it could be 1825: it's as if Constable's *Hay Wain* has been transposed into the era of Fairport Convention. Roger loved these surviving remnants of traditional farming practice, the way that its skills and techniques – such as hedgelaying and tree-pollarding – seemed to be perfectly in step with the rhythms of the natural world. Absent from these older methods were the herbicides and pesticides that stripped the verges, meadows and hedgerows of the species he had learned about on school field trips to the New Forest in the late 1950s.

It wasn't long, however, before bigger and more powerful machines, capable of bringing greater yields without the need for large numbers of labourers, reached the area. In vast, productive fields – bereft of outmoded inconveniences like hedges, footpaths and droving tracks – local landowners saw a brighter and more affluent future. Birds, wild flowers and other denizens of these centuries-old features of the Suffolk landscape would simply have to find new homes elsewhere. It was an attitude that was widespread

Jenny and the Fordson tractor with plough attached, moatside, winter 1973–74.

A hard winter in the early 1980s: the roof of the shepherd's hut is just visible in the left background.

LIFE AT WALNUT TREE FARM

in the postwar period: there was so much countryside to go round – surely a little trimming here and there wouldn't hurt? And it is, perhaps, too easy for us, in this environmentally anxious age, to ignore what must have been the considerable appeal – for farmers weary of back-breaking, labour-intensive and not always dependable ways of producing crops – of new methods that promised reliable yields year after year. The programme of hedge clearance and ditch filling got into its stride in the 1960s, but its terrible downsides – habitat loss, soil erosion and local species extinction, to name but a few – would not become fully apparent for decades, by which time much of the damage was irreversible.

Roger's purchase of the four fields that make up the twelve acres of Walnut Tree Farm at the beginning of the 1970s happened just in time. A few years later the house would have been pulled down and the hedges torn out and replaced by big fields of the kind that surround the farm today.

The patchwork of small fields beyond the farm had been lost a few years earlier. This area included part of Cowpasture Lane, a six-mile drovers' lane – or 'long green' – dating back to the Middle Ages, which linked the local markets at Burgate, Redgrave and Botesdale to Thornham Magna on the main Ipswich-to-Norwich road. A section of this ancient way remained intact, running south from Mellis Common and along Walnut Tree Farm's south-western edge. The land incorporating the lane was bought by the owner

Travellers' horses grazing Cowpasture Lane, late 1990s.

Tree felling on Cowpasture
Lane just before the Tree
Preservation Order came into
force, January 1981.

of the neighbouring farm in 1979 and he soon made known his intention to remove the trees and hedges, and plough up the lane as he had already done on a section south of the railway line. The lane, which varied in width from 30 to 105 feet with hedges on either side, was home to a rich variety of plant species: small wild-flowers including primrose, stitchwort and violet; fruit trees such as blackthorn, wild plum and bullace, as well as mature oak and ash. By design, Cowpasture Lane acted as a corridor or highway for animal species moving between open fields in the wider landscape.

The previous year, 1978, Roger had left Diss Grammar School to join the staff of the environmental organization Friends of the Earth. Here he edited and co-wrote publications, managed press relations and media strategy and planned campaigns. In January 1981 he applied – successfully – for a Tree Preservation Order to protect Cowpasture Lane from destruction. However, word of the impending action must have reached the neighbouring farmer, because, the day before he was served with the Preservation Order, he sent in a wrecking gang, equipped with chainsaws and heavy earth-moving machinery. Roger tried to reason with them, but not before violence had been done to trees, bushes and age-old oaks, so he decided to up the ante by calling in the press. Their arrival on the scene, wielding microphones and cameras, brought the threat to Cowpasture Lane to the attention of a wider public. Over the following months the case for protection of the old drove

One of the many newspaper articles on the battle for Cowpasture Lane, 1981.

LIFE AT WALNUT TREE FARM

ANCIENT WOODLAND UNDER THE AXE

THE sound of a chainsaw and a pall of smoke signalled a severe blow to an ancient piece of woodland on Cowpasture Lane, Mellis on Sunday and Monday just before a tree preservation order was imposed by Mid Suffolk District Council.

A large section of the ancient roadway was cleared of bushes and trees — including oaks 12 inches thick — villagers are angry about the farmer's action.

But, says the farmer Mr William Battell, he was acting within the law in cutting down the trees. He claimed that nothing in the lane is worth preserving, and a government inspector has said so.

A tree preservation order imposed last year was contested by Mr Battell who managed to have the order cancelled by the Secretary of State for the Environment. The Secretary of State for the Environment.

Mr Battell denied that he had moved in with the chainsaw to beat the order. He said he had been cutting in the lane for about three weeks.

Changes in the law now give more power to district councils. Tree preservation orders no longer have to be confirmed by central government. Appeals, however, still go to the Secretary of State.

Mr Battell refused, at first, to talk about the felling on Monday with an *Express* reporter. But later he gave the assurance that, as soon as the tree preservation order was imposed, felling would stop. And he kept his word. He did say, however, that he would take legal advice about appealing against it once again.

The idea of the felling, he said, was to clear the trees so the acre-and-a-half of land between Mellis Common and the railway line could be brought under the plough.

On the far side of the line a portion of the footpath leading to Thornham Magna has already been ploughed up by Mr Battell. But Mr Battell conceded, the public had the right to walk across his crops which obstruct their way at this point.

The very wide footpath contained a dense growth of many varieties of trees and plants and, says Mr Battell, his crops have been severely damaged by rabbits which lurk in the belt of woodland.

Mr Roger Deakin who lives at the Mellis end of the footpath at Walnut Tree Farm is a parish councillor who has actively campaigned to keep the historic path, part of the old market highway from Thornham to Botesdale. He was at the scene on Monday trying to persuade Mr Battell, his son Nigel and the workmen to stop work.

He sees the lane as a unique part of the Suffolk heritage and points out that very few areas of woodland of this antiquity now survive.

He told the *Express:* "The fact that the landowner has cut down many of the trees is, of course, regrettable but it is only a temporary set back in the long life of Cowpasture Lane whose boundary hedges and trees have probably been coppiced at regular intervals since medieval times."

Another villager Mr Gordon Smith was saddened by Mr Battell's action. "It is regrettable that he seems to have jumped the gun," he said.

Mr John Shackles of the Nature Conservancy Council also regretted the loss. "I think it is pretty irresponsible for a landowner to do this if he knows a tree preservation order is about to be imposed."

The preservation order which was served on the owner of the land Mr Nigel Battell on Monday afternoon was authorised last Friday.

COWPASTURE Lane as it has been for many years . . . a wide footpath and home for many species of flora and fauna.

Chief planner of Mid Suffolk District Council Mr Bernard Horstead said several letters supporting the preservation had been received. He had also had representations from the Friends of the Earth and the Suffolk Preservation Society.

District and county councillor Mr Guy MacGregor, who stressed the tremendous amenity and historic value of the area, said the highway authority should be urged to take action to reinstate the public right of way which has been ploughed up.

Following a report in a national newspaper on Wednesday where Mr Battell was quoted as saying: "It is my land and I am entitled to do what I want with it. You were too late," Mr Battell denied that he had said anything of the kind.

"I would never dream of saying a thing like that," he said.

But, he told the *Express:* "The council should take the lane over or maintain it. I am prepared to sell them the lane provided I have a right of way through it."

WILDLIFE

COWPASTURE Lane has been a home for:

Trees: Dogwood, field maple, hazel, oak, ash, sallow, blackthorn, hawthorn, elm (very little of this "modern" species) elder, holly and spindle tree.

Plants: Honeysuckle, dogs mercury, nettle-leaved bellflower, dogrose, bryony, primrose, cowslip, cranesbill, cuckoo pint, bluebell, etc.

Birds: Nightingale, tree creeper, lesser spotted woodpecker, green woodpecker, long tailed tit, coal tit, wren, goldfinch, willow warbler, tawny owl, etc.

Path of history

COWPASTURE Lane is part of the old market road running from Thornham, through Mellis and Burgate (where it is known as Furze Way) to Botesdale. Over much of its length (in fact all of its length in the parish of Thornham Parva) it is in a state of preservation as an ancient lane.

Thornham Magna's north-east boundary was set along it, a clear indication that it was in being in the very early middle ages. Burgate Redgrave and Botesdale all had grants of a market in the 13th century and the lane would have been very busy at that time.

When the railway was cut through the lane in the 19th century it was described as "pasture and lane" through which there is a right of way. This right of pasture suggests that the lane was not only a right of way but also one of the "long greens".

Using M. D. Hooper's method number of tree and bush species in a 30 yards stretch and multiplying by 100 — the lane is at least 900 years old.

The dominance in the lane of dogwood, field maple and hazel, associated with woodland flora such as dog's mercury and nettle-leaved bellflower, and the richness and variety of tree and coppice species, suggests that the lane contains relics of the pre-Doomsday wildwood.

Old people in Mellis believe the lane is part of the Roman road. This could be the embroidery of folklore, but it helps to indicate the age of the lane.

If the rootstock were to be removed, a possibility that still remains if the landowner should win an appeal against the tree preservation order, nothing could replace what history and nature have created there.

COWPASTURE Lane . . . after the chain-saw.

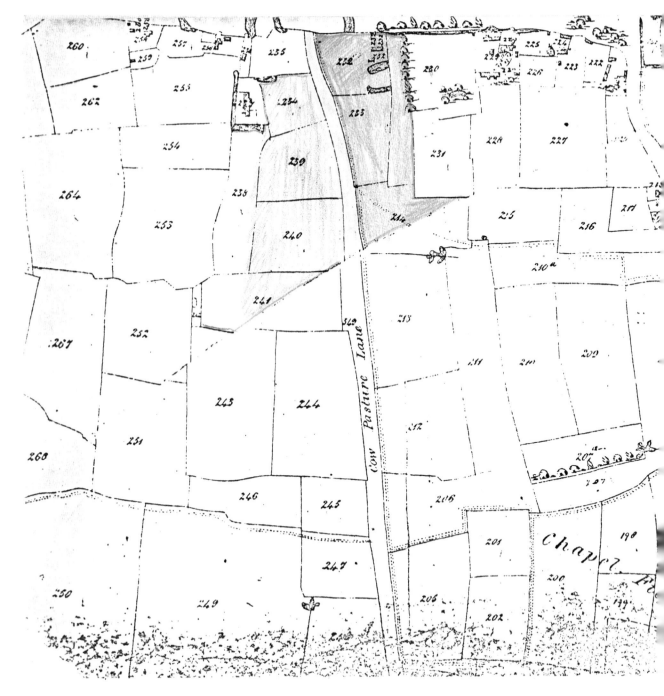

Map used in the legal fight against the attempt to overturn the Tree Preservation Order: Walnut Tree Farm land is in red, Cowpasture Lane in green, trees damaged in yellow, and defendant's land in blue. Much of the medieval field structure and many of the hedges shown on the map have been removed since the 1950s.

IN THE HIGH COURT OF JUSTICE

QUEEN'S BENCH DIVISION

1981. A. No.

BETWEEN:

THE ATTORNEY GENERAL, AT THE RELATION

OF ROGER STEWART DEAKIN (THE RELATOR)   First Plaintiff

- and -

ROGER STEWART DEAKIN   Second Plaintiff

- and -

WILLIAM BATTELL   Defendant

AFFIDAVIT

I, Roger Stewart Deakin, of Walnut Tree Farm, Melliss, Eye, Suffolk MAKE OATH AND SAY as follows:

1. I am the Second Plaintiff and the Relator herein. I crave leave to refer to the Statement of Claim herein. The facts and matters set out in paragraphs 1 to 5 thereof are true.

2. There is now produced and shown to me marked "R.S.D. 1" a map showing my land (in red), the highway (in green) and the Defendant's land (in blue).

3. Cow Pasture Lane is a highway and right of way of great antiquity and is of both historical and environmental interest and value. It is an old market lane and the total length is some six miles. At the point in issue it varies in width between 90 and 35 feet and is bounded by coppice

-1-

road gained vigorous support – a petition was signed and letters written. By June 1981 the High Court had ruled in favour of the Tree Preservation Order – a significant early victory in the ongoing campaign to protect the British countryside from the depredations of agribusiness. The court order gave Cowpasture Lane protection for the next twenty-five years, but over this period Roger had to work hard to ensure that its legal status remained unthreatened and that it was properly managed. Proposals to trim back the tree line bordering the field adjacent to the lane were always subjected to his close scrutiny, and were always followed up promptly with letters and by consultations with local landowners and the appropriate authorities.

The section of the lane scrubbed out in the late 1960s remained ploughed up well into the early 2000s and since then has been grudgingly left as a six-foot-wide strip of grass that is regularly burned back by weedkiller. Reinstating the missing section would require little effort, and the zeitgeist is surely favourable – the casual ecological vandalism of past decades having been replaced by more sustainable attitudes to land management. With the fiftieth anniversary of the grubbing-out approaching, the earth movers could easily put back what was torn out half a century before. A modern excavator could dig out the ditches and level the spoil in a few days, and the planting of saplings would create a framework for nature to build on.

Affidavit sworn by Roger, relating to the legal attempt to overturn the Cowpasture Lane Tree Preservation Order.

ABOVE
The regeneration of
Cowpasture Lane, late 1980s.

ABOVE RIGHT
Roger maintaining fields
around the farm, early 2000s.

RIGHT
Beyond the railway line:
the missing section of
Cowpasture Lane, removed
in 1970.

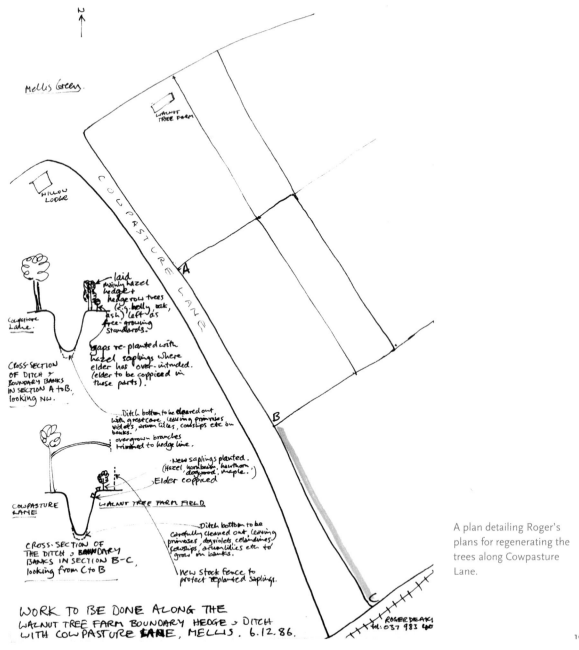

Mellis Green.

WALNUT TREE FARM

WILLOW LODGE

COWPASTURE LANE

A

laid mainly hazel hedge + hedgerow trees (e.g. holly, oak, ash) left as free-growing standards.

gaps re-planted with hazel saplings where elder has over-intruded. (elder to be coppiced in these parts).

Cowpasture Lane.

CROSS-SECTION OF DITCH + BOUNDARY BANKS IN SECTION A to B. looking NW.

Ditch bottom to be cleared out, with great care, leaving primroses, violets, arum lilies, cowslips etc on banks.
overgrown branches trimmed to hedge line.

B

New saplings planted. (Hazel, hornbeam, hawthorn, dogwood, maple.)
Elder coppiced

WALNUT TREE FARM FIELD

COWPASTURE LANE

CROSS-SECTION OF THE DITCH + BOUNDARY BANKS IN SECTION B-C, looking from C to B.

Ditch bottom to be carefully cleaned out, leaving primroses, dog violets, celandines, cowslips, arum lilies etc. to grow on banks.

New stock fence to protect replanted saplings.

C

ROGER DEAKIN
tel: 037 983 400

WORK TO BE DONE ALONG THE WALNUT TREE FARM BOUNDARY HEDGE + DITCH WITH COWPASTURE LANE, MELLIS. 6.12.86.

A plan detailing Roger's plans for regenerating the trees along Cowpasture Lane.

CHAPTER 4

Barns, Wagons, Sheds and Sculpture

I have a weakness for sheds or huts of all kinds

WILDWOOD

THE VARIOUS STRUCTURES DOTTED AROUND Walnut Tree Farm were (and remain) spaces for living, sleeping, reading, writing and travelling. Many of them – barns, sheds, shepherds' huts, a railway wagon, the timber-framed Morgan (not to mention the frame of the house itself) were fashioned from wood. The versatility and beauty of wood never failed to fascinate and delight Roger; almost anything wooden was of interest to him.

Work on the house was finished by the mid-1970s, but every farm needs a barn. The first modest construction, built behind the walnut tree, was put together easily enough using salvaged timbers and tin. Soon afterwards a small seventeenth-century barn that was surplus to a local farmer's needs was disassembled and brought to the farm. The dismantling took only a few days but, like the rebuilding of the house, the re-erection of a partially rotten timber frame required considerably more effort. Friends and skilled local tradesmen pitched in again and the building was eventually completed, after a fashion.* The resulting structure was used as a tractor shed, workshop and hayloft.

This was not the last of Roger's barn rescues. When he learned that a large two-storey barn nearby was to be demolished to make

PREVIOUS SPREAD
Roger re-erects the second
barn, mid-1980s.

* Once Roger had drawn what he wanted, creatively speaking, from a particular task or activity, he tended to lose the impetus to 'finish' it in any conventional sense of the word.

The first barn, built by Roger and Serena from reclaimed materials in the early 1980s.

Serena tries the first barn
for size.

Roger knocks pegs into the
frame of the second barn.

LIFE AT WALNUT TREE FARM

BARNS, WAGONS, SHEDS AND SCULPTURE

way for a modern prefab, he resolved to save the eighteenth-century building. The principal timbers, joists, rafters and purlins* were broken up into kit form and transported to Walnut Tree Farm. A base for the transplanted structure, measuring some 65 feet by 22 feet, was laid with brick footings. However, his ambitious plan to re-erect the old barn did not come to fruition. Work on the frame stalled at the laborious de-nailing stage, at which point the component parts were stacked at the edge of the field and left there.

---

* A horizontal beam along the length of a roof, resting on principals and supporting the common rafters or boards.

RIGHT
Scattered components of the barn. The working method was 'make it up as you go along'.

OPPOSITE
One of the challenges of working with ancient timbers is that they can conceal old nails, waiting to wreck a sharp blade.

112   LIFE AT WALNUT TREE FARM

The frame of the first barn complete, and ready for its tin roof.

The first timbers go down on the second barn. In the background is a heavily laden tractor trailer, with a railway wagon behind it.

RIGHT
A view of the finished second barn from the common, late 1980s.

OPPOSITE
A view from the barn workshop through reclaimed windows to field and railway wagon outside.

Anna, daughter of Roger's friend Margot, marches off to work between walnut tree and second barn, armed with a pitchfork, mid-1990s.

LIFE AT WALNUT TREE FARM

Brambles soon took hold, and the deconstructed barn was swallowed into the hedge where it remains to this day – a fungus-covered stockade frequented by local foxes.

Not all of the structures that arrived at the farm were as large as this. Smaller and lighter constructions – woodsheds and huts for goats and chickens among them – became features of the landscape of the farm. Then in 1980 came a real find. At nearby South Lopham, just over the county boundary in Norfolk, someone was getting rid of a down-at-heel shepherd's hut. Just like the house itself, the utilitarian wagon was ripe for rejuvenation. New timbers were let in, weatherboard replaced, windows repaired and a wood-burner installed. The floor was covered with threadbare Persian rugs, and a pine table and bed with horsehair mattress completed the furnishings. Roger parked the hut on the far side of the moat – a couple of hundred yards from the house and just visible from the front door – its curved tin roof silhouetted against the eastern sky.

Hard on the heels of this mobile home in the meadow came a Depression-era goods wagon, of the type ridden by the panhandlers and hobos whose travails inspired the ballads of Woody Guthrie. Weighing in at around two tonnes after the undercarriages were removed, with double skin hardwood boards, barrel roof and steel bracing, the wagon was lifted by crane onto waiting brick piles next to one of the ponds between the farm and the common. A wood-burner, rug and bed were all that was needed to transform

OPPOSITE
The shepherd's hut on its way to Walnut Tree Farm, delivered by tractor and trailer, October 1980.

The shepherd's hut finally arrives, signs of wear and tear clearly visible.

RIGHT
The shepherd's hut repaired
and in position, winter
1980–81. A fresh coat of paint
would have to wait for the
warmer weather.

OPPOSITE
Painted and warming in the
morning sun, the shepherd's
hut in the early 1980s.

Abandoned railway wagons
captured by Roger's camera
(though these ones never
made it as far as Walnut
Tree Farm).

the bare interior into a simple but homely room. Thanks to its sliding door, guests and residents can enjoy starry nights here, or wake to the sight of the sun rising across the meadow.

As he had done with the timbers of the unreconstructed barn, Roger secreted his collection of salvaged wood in places around the farm – under old sheets of corrugated tin, in rusted and abandoned cars, in sheds overgrown with brambles. Pillaged from skips, clearance auctions and building sites, and ferried home on the roof of his large Citroën, Roger's inventory of rescued woodwork was immense and heterogeneous, but always purposeful. In one shed, for instance, he stored a large collection of sash windows. Making windows requires both skill and time, so, when building a new shed, why not just take an old sash and make the wall fit the window, rather than the other way round? Another rescued item, a full-sized, but dismantled and scattered Victorian church organ, was, on the face of it, a challenging object to reuse. But its individual mechanical components, almost all of them wooden, some of them coated in graphite and scored or pierced in elaborate designs, were successfully repurposed as shelves or headboards.

Many other activities in the workshop centred on working with wood – turning, carving, sometimes with a chainsaw. Chairs, desks, shelves, beds and lamps were fashioned from raw timber or juxtapositions of dissimilar man-made objects brought together to make interesting and functional one-offs.

The garden table on the moat side of the farm, just about hanging on.

It is no great surprise, given his passion for wood, that Roger planted hundreds of trees: on home territory, and sometimes just beyond, on the common or by Cowpasture Lane. He allowed hedges to expand upwards and outwards. The wood that he and his then partner Serena planted in 1987, in part of the railway line field, comprised some 200 saplings of ash, oak, hornbeam and field maple.

Older trees in danger of toppling over or losing a major limb would be propped up by large elm forks fashioned from the young elm trees. These trees, which had succumbed to Dutch elm disease, could be found around the farm: their hard and sinuous wood was ideal for the task and gave the supported trees a Daliesque appearance.

Roger's love of trees also found expression in sculptural projects. Impressed by the Ash Dome that the sculptor David Nash had planted in Wales in 1977, he planted eight ash saplings in two rows and allowed them to grow to a size at which they could be pleached together to form a long archway or bower. Over the years the branches fused to become one tree with eight trunks. Other single trees, often ash, were sculpted into peculiar forms with stakes and rope.

In the autumn the fallen yellow leaves of the white mulberry tree were gathered into a maze-like puzzle in a style akin to that of

The David Nash-inspired ash bower after the first weaving together of the eight saplings.

Ice tower and arch in the style of Roger's friend and collaborator Andy Goldsworthy.

LIFE AT WALNUT TREE FARM

ABOVE
'The ash arch is sending out shoots. The laid hedge of the wood is bursting into fresh green leaf,' wrote Roger in a 7 May journal entry.

ABOVE RIGHT
Cherry tree 'ball'.

RIGHT
'Lily's Maze': a mulberry leaf maze, again inspired by Andy Goldsworthy.

Andy Goldsworthy, who had collaborated with Roger on projects outside the farm. In the depths of winter another Goldsworthy-inspired activity was to take small slabs of ice, two or three inches thick, and stack them in a single tower, or two leaning towers, until they formed a fragile arch.

A common theme connects these activities: all of them demonstrate elements of transition or transformation. The ash bower moves from the natural world to that of artistic expression. The ice arch will soon melt away. A tree sapling has multiple and near-infinite possible incarnations ahead of it. And, provided it is not burnt, the decaying trunk of a dead tree will support a multitude of species. The decomposition of things is evident around the farm and its prominence is unlikely to be accidental. The sheds constructed and filled over the 1970s and onwards became more and more decrepit. Blanketed with rotting leaves, the corrugated tin rusted through and eventually gave way, collapsing in on itself to merge with the sheds' contents beneath. Brambles then engulfed the structures, deterring human intrusion.

Watching this slow process of decay, this passage from our world to wilderness, was a quiet joy and inspiration for Roger. Since his passing, the majority of these structures have continued to sink back into the land, only occasionally disturbed by an intruder looking for a suitable window or piece of timber for some other project.

The wood planted in 1987 by Roger and Serena in the railway field, coming along well after a few years of growth.

CHAPTER 5

The Moat

Very bright blue frosty day. Moat and ponds
properly frozen for the first time this year.

NOTES FROM WALNUT TREE FARM,
'DECEMBER'

T HE MOAT AT WALNUT TREE FARM IS FED BY a spring, a reliable source of water that may well be the reason why the original sixteenth-century builders of the farm decided to raise a single-storey timber frame here. 'There is a spring in the moat… below the surface,' Roger wrote, 'and it never lets the moat dry up or even lose its level much beyond a slight rising and falling of the tide with the seasons.' He sensed the significance of the moat from his first encounter with the ruined house: 'I am part-islanded by a moat,' runs an entry in one of his notebooks. 'I have perhaps also earned some kinship with the people who built the house, and probably dug out the moat by hand, 450 years ago.'

Roger's notebooks also record the initial clearing of branches from in and around the moat: he speaks of 'dragging out huge roots of dead old willows'. Later he and others would capture its changing humours from season to season in innumerable photographs. A hard winter in the early 1980s froze the ice so thick that a table was laid for twelve in the middle of the moat. Guests enjoyed a fine lunch in the winter sun, until a seismic crack was heard from beneath the table, prompting some to leap from their chairs and hurry for the bank, while other – calmer – souls remained seated.

It was only really after 1990 that people began to swim in the moat. In that year the Suffolk Wildlife Trust, which had recently received as a bequest the area of Mellis Common that belonged

LIFE AT WALNUT TREE FARM

142

Summer reflections in the
moat in the late 1980s, before
it was dredged.

The moat during Roger's first
winter at the farm, 1970–71.

ABOVE
The heavy dredging machinery used to scoop out centuries' worth of silt and debris from the bottom of the moat, February 1990.

ABOVE RIGHT
The thorough clear-out gave the moat a depth of around ten feet at high water in the spring.

RIGHT
Water steadily returning, spring 1990.

ABOVE
The moat after a spring
snowfall, 1990.

LEFT
The moat in late autumn,
1990.

Winter 1990–91: Roger tests
the thickness of the ice.

to Lord Henniker,* undertook a programme of pond and ditch clearing. The complex system of common drainage devised in medieval times had long been neglected. The Trust contracted heavy dredging and digging machinery to carry out the works, which included a section of the common in front of Walnut Tree Farm. When Roger saw the heavy caterpillar-tracked machinery creeping along the frontage, he sensed an opportunity: for a reasonable sum, could not the works make a small detour, and scoop out hundreds of years' worth of silt and debris from the moat? In due course the water was professionally pumped out and several tons of artefact-laden silt removed and spread over the adjacent field. The spoils consisted of scores of old glass jars and bottles, together with pieces of broken crockery tossed into the moat by generations of residents, the embossed names of long-forgotten brands of jam, marmalade, lemonade and beer encrusted in mud.

The dredging was carried out in January and February to minimize its impact on aquatic species, and the waters soon returned. Cleared of slime and rubbish, the moat's average depth along its centre line was now around ten feet, its waters limpid and unclogged by weed (though they would not remain so for long). Its potential as a natural swimming pool was immediately apparent. Roger began

---

* John Patrick Edward Chandos Henniker-Major, 8th Baron Henniker, was a distinguished civil servant and diplomat whose ancestral seat was at Thornham Hall, near Eye.

to take regular swims in the moat, and the habit soon caught on with his friends, enticed by reports of the invigorating effects of immersion in its fresh, cool waters. Roger's long and easy strokes across the moat would soon turn to the stroke of pen on paper. He was inspired to make a 'swimmer's journey through Britain' and thereafter to write a book about it. *Waterlog*, published in 1999, encouraged a nascent movement of wild swimmers to take to Britain's rivers, lakes and lidos – and even the odd whirlpool.

Under Roger's relaxed, chemical-free stewardship, the moat – like the fields and hedges that surround it – flourished and prospered. Plant and animal life responded with an explosion of

growth. The weed flora, crucial for oxygenation and home to dozens of water-borne species, multiplied exponentially. Soon there was too much to permit a decent swimming stroke: the weeds' long tendrils would coil around arm or leg – at best inconveniencing the swimmer, at worst threatening to pull them below the surface and into the domain of newt, frog and freshwater snail.

To end this state of affairs and facilitate the serious business of swimming, Roger used a dinghy as a platform from which to pull up the long filaments of weed growing from the moat bed. The fore and aft decks of the dinghy were soon piled as high as the fishing nets of a sampan on the Yangtze delta. A variety of creatures came up with the weed, and the boat's cargo would be decanted to the bank to let these accidental stowaways crawl, hop or slither home.

Sometimes Roger managed to combine swimming with weed-clearance: 'After scything and working up a sweat,' he wrote in a fragment that found its way into *Notes from Walnut Tree Farm*, 'cleared out the Canadian pondweed, hugging armfuls of it to my breast and breaststroking one-armed to the bank.'

Just as growth on dry land died back at the end of the summer, so it was in the moat. Winter swims, therefore – however bracing – were not hindered by rampant plant life, which by now had retreated to the depths. There are those who like to swim in temperatures scarcely above freezing wearing only a pair of Speedos, but Roger was not among them. A neoprene wetsuit, dark and shiny, may

Roger takes a punt in a clinker-built dinghy, mid-1990s.

THIS PAGE
Roger with some amphibian
friends.

OVERLEAF
Notes for a BBC Radio 4
radio documentary,
The House.

have lent him a passing resemblance to a giant newt, but it made it possible to have a proper cold-weather swim, rather than a brief and unhappy encounter between icy water and goose-pimpled skin.

In fact, the newts so dear to Roger's heart are fair-weather swimmers, only taking to the water in the warmer months to socialize, hunt and mate. They wrap their fertilized eggs in a pond leaf envelope and seal them with a loving kiss of egg glue. Come the chillier months, the newts retreat beneath rotting logs or flagstones to hibernate. Some of them go the extra mile and seek out resting places inside the house, emerging in the spring wearing thick fur coats of fluff. Just as Roger donned a shape-shifting newtsuit to swim in their waterworld, so the newts executed their own change of clothes in the dry environment of the house. When Roger noticed a creeping fluff ball he would scoop it up and air-ambulance the newt to the moat's edge. After a moment's hydrotherapy the heavy winter coat would fall away and another season of pool parties could get underway. However, the occasional discovery of a dried and shrunken salamandrine body was poignant proof that not every newt survived the winter indoors to ply once more the waters of the moat.

RD|NOTE|5
THE HOUSE chapter -notes

While the rest of the world has seems to have played a increasingly boisterous game of musical chairs all around me, I have stayed put in the same house for thirty-five years. It sits on the shores of a great inland sea of rippling grasses that rises like a tide towards July, obscuring my neighbour's farm on its opposite side rim. It is a value a mile to the west of this place my gate and is said to be the most extensive grazing common in Suffolk. So although the sea is twenty-five miles due east at Walberswick, I can enjoy some of the pleasures of living by it: The big skies and wide, dramatic sunsets. In Suffolk, we have volcanic cumulus clouds instead of mountains and explore their snowy crags in daydreams.

I live at a dizzy 174 feet above sea level, enough to keep the place islanded when the promised flood comes. But I am part-islanded already by a moat and a round pond that juts into the anymoor which is felt partially moated. The jungled hedges and ditches that surround my four meadows comprise a necessary rampart to the great prairies beyond, winds that cut across the wheat prairies beyond. There's a wood, too and an old droving road, a green lane they too are volcanic, erupting with ~~~~ each spring.

Why have I stayed so long? The place was a ruin when I found it in 1969. ~~~~~~ ~~~~~~ ~~~~~~ ~~~~~~ I noticed a chimney rising out of the spinney of ~~was~~ blackthorn and brambles ~~that forged the commons~~ and went to investigate. The place was a ruin, not much considered by old Arthur, ~~lorens~~ who ~~owned it and~~ kept pigs in it downstairs, ~~and~~ chickens ~~on the floor up~~ upstairs. The roof was a patchwork of ~~~~ corrugated iron and ~~~~ gently composting thatch. I love ruins because they are always doing what everything ~~too~~ really wants to do all the time: returning ~~themselves~~ to the earth, ~~becoming part of the~~ ~~~~ melting back into the landscape. ~~~~ ~~~~ ~~~~ ~~wandering that night I studied the~~ ~~~~ 2½ inch map, and ~~realised~~ ~~~~ ~~location~~ confirmed how ~~~~~ ideally ~~~~ secluded ~~~~ the house was, and ~~~~ Arthur consented to sell me the house, and we went on to become the best of friends, even sharing Heather, a ~~~~ Guernsey ~~cow~~ house-cow, for a while.

~~~~ Slowly, I ~~~~ stripped the house to its skeleton of oak, chestnut, and ash ~~~~ and repaired it with old timbers gleaned from a barm the farmers took down. I ~~~~ lived in the back of a Volkswagen van for a while, then ~~camped out in parts of~~ ~~the parts of the house I wasn't~~ ~~~~ made a bivouac against the ~~~~ big ~~~~ central fireplace and slept beside ~~~~ the wood fire with the cats for

company. ~~Later~~ In spring, I moved upstairs into what
felt like a treehouse, ~~with the stars sleeping~~
under the stars in ~~.....~~
and ~~.....~~ bed with a rigged canvas roof and
walls. soon, the woodpigeons in the ash tree
at eye level grew used to me, and ~~strutted~~
~~its ..... overhanging branches~~ unself-
~~consciously. we were ..... on terms of the~~
~~greatest intimacy~~

~~I think ..... it is~~ Having
~~to~~ repaired and ~~rebuilt~~ re-made the house
myself, I ~~..... on terms~~ of the greatest
intimacy with every ~~..... beam and~~
post and pegged joint in the place'. ~~.....~~
~~..... I have ..... is .....~~
~~..... originally~~ I have perhaps also
earned some kinships with the people who
built the house and probably dug out the
moat by hand, #50 years ago. ~~I think~~
~~many people never truly take possession of their~~
~~houses. To do so you must ..... but only~~
with a great deal of work, and love, can
you truly 'take possession' of a house.
— But here I want to catch
myself out, because "take possession" is itself
revealing of an outdated attitude to ~~houses~~
and land.

imagine a house.

157

3

EFFORT AND REWAR

I love ruins because they are always doing what everything always wants to do all the time: returning to the earth, melting back into the landscape.

WILDWOOD

ROGER PASSED AWAY BESIDE THE CENTRAL fireplace at Walnut Tree Farm in August 2006. In accordance with his wishes the farm was mothballed for twelve months, after which his personal possessions were moved out and my family and I moved in and life carried on. Although his physical presence had left the farm, Roger was palpable in every corner of the house, in the barns and sheds, and in the landscape.

In September 2009, his writing notes, journals, manuscripts, documentary film-making rushes, photographs and assorted ephemera (including a pair of old swimming trunks) were donated to the Roger Deakin archive at the University of East Anglia.

Outside the house, Roger's vast collection of wooden objects, building materials, farm machinery and rusting Citroën DS Safaris – together with items whose use was indeterminate but which were interesting to him in design or construction – remained in place, either exposed to the elements or hidden under old tin sheets and in mouldering sheds.

Whenever we discovered a buried item, I would make a mental note of its potential usefulness on the one hand, and its frailty and vulnerability on the other. This mental inventory – a 'map of things' – existed in a permanent state of flux: as the sheds and vehicles and their contents become more overgrown and more rotten, their serviceability diminished in inverse proportion to their

ABOVE LEFT
The kitchen at Walnut Tree
Farm, late 2006.

ABOVE RIGHT
One of many bookcases at
the farm holding Roger's
library, late 2006.

RIGHT
One of Roger's desks as it
was left in the year the house
was mothballed

ABOVE
Inside the cab of the BMC
pick-up truck, 2017.

OPPOSITE
Wild hops take hold of
the truck.

decrepitude. The eternal dilemma of what to preserve and what to abandon was influenced by the cycle of nature and the incidence of chance discovery. When new relics – whether tractor implements, 78rpm records or bottles of home-brewed cider – came to light, the inventory's internal hierarchy underwent further shifts. Some discoveries proved beyond repair and were left as they were found, to melt into the wilderness and provide a home for plants and animals. Leaving the Citroëns and collapsing sheds alone and forgetting what is in them, means one job less to think about.

External and interior views of one of the three Citroën, DS Safaris. Parked or, perhaps more accurately, 'hedged', the cars are obscured by the thick brambles and nettles that thrive on the minerals leaching from their rusting hulks.

A farm trailer nearly beyond repair. The home-made design using truck wheels and rudimentary recycled components is typical of 1950s agri-manufacture.

ABOVE
Zig-zag harrows ready to
level molehills and aerate
the meadow grass that has
'thatched' over winter.

ABOVE RIGHT
Another Citroën, DS in
deep cover.

RIGHT
A nine-tine harrow.

LEFT
A shed built by Roger from salvaged tin. The sheets may be the ones that kept the rain out in his first winter at the farm.

ABOVE LEFT
A collection of old 78s, at home in the leaf litter.

ABOVE LEFT
Useful contents of a hedgerow shed: chairs, sash windows and organ pipes.

A bullock cart, just about
defying gravity.

ABOVE RIGHT
The boom of a hay mower,
as seen in use on page 80.

OPPOSITE
Cast-iron railing ornaments,
unearthed near the 78rpm
record collection.

More sash windows, beams and furniture stashed away for future construction or renovation.

And there's quite enough on the 'to do' list already... But it's good to know they are there – and good to keep a bit of Rog around, for old times' sake.

In taking on Walnut Tree Farm, we had also inherited a sizeable community outside its physical boundaries. Many people have strong feelings of connection with the house and land, either directly, as friends of Roger's, or indirectly, through acquaintance with his work in the environmental movement and associated film projects – or simply through love of his books. These feelings cover a wide emotional spectrum. Stepping into Roger's shoes – or rather his Wellingtons – comes with a responsibility to navigate the sea of emotions that can sometimes roll in at storm force 10 but which usually ripples more gently in the breeze.

A balance has to be struck between preserving and restoring what Roger created, and developing or evolving it. Many of the tasks around the farm require strenuous physical input and, just as Roger enlisted skilled help from his neighbours (forging relation-ships that went far beyond a cold exchange of cash for labour), so did we. The work is such that aching backs and numb fingers are an unavoidable and sometimes demoralizing accompaniment. But the end results make the pain and sweat worthwhile – the rewards always outweigh the effort.

CHAPTER 6

Roofing, repairing, dredging, wood-cutting

… my cosy cabin is a shepherd's hut
in the lee of a south-facing Suffolk hedge.

WILDWOOD

B Y THE LATE 2000S, MUCH OF THE FABRIC OF the farm had returned to, or was approaching, the ruinous state in which Roger had first found it back in 1969.

Two years after we moved in to the house, the deterioration of the shepherd's hut had reached a tipping point. It was still just about habitable, but it bore the imprint of annual batterings by wind and rain: a storm had destroyed one of the four small side windows, while the larger window at the rear – half of a Victorian sash no doubt salvaged from a skip – was collapsing. An old tarpaulin had been roped around the gable end to keep the worst of the weather out. With winter approaching and the inevitable saturation of the exposed wood transforming sound timbers to mulch, we prised the tired shiplap boards, rotten windows and frilled tin away from the frame. The tin, rolled from heavy-gauge steel and only superficially rusty, could go back on, but the boards and side windows needed to be remade from scratch. A decade earlier, Roger had laid up a large block of beech under some tin to season, which would provide enough timber to make the four small windows. The sills would be fashioned from a similar piece of oak.

Brian McGuinness's roving days had come to an end and he now lay over the common in St Mary's churchyard. We found his successor, 'Mad' Dave Towill, three houses away from Walnut Tree Farm, rebuilding his own timber-framed house – a structure every bit as dilapidated as Roger's had been in 1970. A skilled carpenter

ABOVE LEFT
Twenty-eight years after
its previous repairs in 1980,
the shepherd's hut was in
a fragile state.

ABOVE RIGHT
The hut stripped back to
repair the frame.

RIGHT
Insulation!

The hut repaired: new boards have been fitted on the sides, and a sash window from a nearby shed installed at its back end. The boards around the sash window are originals that remained sound.

The shepherd's hut in the middle field before repair, summer 2008.

and general builder specializing in old houses – and soon-to-be friend – Dave was working on his house in between carrying out repairs on others in the area, but he still found the time to provide the skilled guidance we needed in order to rescue the hut. In his workshop he turned the rough blocks of beech and oak into beautifully finished frames and sills. We sent a sample of the old shiplap to a toolmaker, so that cutting blades could be ground to the profile required to run off new boards. Roger's sash window collection in one of the corrugated tin sheds turned up a solid example of almost the same dimensions as its predecessor.

It was a daunting job compounded by an unpredictable deadline. Sooner or later the weather would turn. Rain and power tools don't make a good combination and the diminishing light would limit the hours available. Under the circumstances, we decided the best approach was to stay optimistic and keep up the momentum of work. We didn't want to have to put the project on hold until the following spring or summer, when another worthy endeavour might muscle its way to the front of the queue, condemning the hut to remain for ever on the 'back burner'. The hut was such a recognizable and enduring feature of the Walnut Tree Farm Roger had created, it seemed wrong to allow it to disintegrate, and for the boards, windows and tin to rot with the Citroëns in the brambles. Luckily, in October 2009 we enjoyed an Indian summer, which allowed us to apply the finishing touches of glass puttying and

OPPOSITE
Winter dawn, viewed from
the hut window.

ROOFING, REPAIRING, DREDGING, WOOD-CUTTING

The roof in 2010, before
it was stripped back to
the frame.

painting before the late autumn rains blew in. Rather than lose the craftsmanship of the window lines and joints by painting over them, we applied a preserving oil instead, which further enhanced their detail. All the interior needed was a good clean: we beat out the rugs, cleared away decades of accumulated cobwebs, and oiled the bare pine panels. Rendered safe from the destructive effects of sun, wind and rain, the hut was ready to welcome guests once more. Occupants can relish being in a space close to nature, but enjoy a comfort level a star or two higher than a tent or bivvy bag.

*

In January 2010, some forty years after its last overhaul, the time had come to replace the farm's tired and leaking roof. We knew that many of the materials needed for the job lay close at hand, buried deep in a hedge. Three thousand five hundred pantiles and one thousand two hundred peg tiles were billeted there, under a covering of rust-holed tin. Whether they had been discarded as surplus after the roof was mended in 1971, or were left over from the uncompleted building of the third barn, no one really knew. But they now saw daylight for the first time in decades, and a full regiment of tiles was mustered to repair the roof. The toads, worms and beetles disturbed by the tiles' sudden mobilization fled their old home for quieter quarters. Those tiles found to be unfit

ABOVE
The roof's north-facing
elevation is a favourable spot
for moss and lichen growth.

RIGHT
Another sunshine-filled East
Anglian day.

FAR RIGHT
Much of the work on the
roof involved fashioning
the lead valleys and cutting
and cementing tiles for the
dormer window roofs.

188

ABOVE LEFT
Most of the pantiles removed from the roof were reusable, and went straight back on; damaged ones were repurposed as pot-hole fillers on the track leading to the common.

ABOVE RIGHT
Modern materials beneath the tiles help reduce the icy draughts entering the house, and keep precious heat in.

for roofing duty were redeployed as pot-hole fillers on the track between the farm and common. The terracotta shards gave the track a pinkish-brown hue, like the russet carpet of The Mall as it unrolls towards Buckingham Palace.

*

Getting the lines right on a roof where nothing is straight or square requires skills honed over many years.

Every autumn the moat, lying a couple of feet below field level and encircled by willow, ash and hazel, receives a substantial share of the leaf-fall. For a few days a patchwork blanket sits on its

LIFE AT WALNUT TREE FARM

The pumped-out moat,
February 2017, revealing the
leaves that had accumulated
since the previous dredging
in 1990.

LIFE AT WALNUT TREE FARM

surface before becoming waterlogged and drifting downwards to join the pondweed dying back after summer's bloom. Over time, the build-up of decaying organic matter in the moat can upset the oxygen and pH levels of the water, inhibiting plant growth and imperilling animal life. By the mid-2010s, a quarter of a century's accumulated leaf-fall was beginning to make its presence felt in other ways. Swimmers in the moat found their nostrils assailed by pungent fumes as their strokes disturbed pockets of sulphurous gas produced by the decomposing weeds and leaves below.

Without a dredging team conveniently at hand, we took a more DIY approach. Choosing a moment in the depths of winter, as Roger had done (to minimize the impact on the remaining wildlife), we hired, for a single day, the services of a friend who was skilled in handling a twenty-ton tracked digger. As had happened twenty-seven years previously, the water was pumped out and the spoil spread on the adjacent field, where it dried to the point where the tractor and zig-zag harrows could level it off and clear it of rocks, large branches and the odd artefact dropped in since 1990. The previous dredge had scooped up most of the ancient items and so very few man-made objects came up this time: just one saucepan – which was returned to kitchen duties immediately – and six mercury thermometers, still intact and presumably lost by Roger when he was monitoring water temperatures. While the moat was empty the spring-water feed was clearly visible on the

south-western bank and it soon returned the moat to its natural level. Thanks to the rejuvenating effects of the clear-out, the following spring and summer of 2017 exceeded all expectations. The moat was alive with dragonflies, damselflies and a myriad other freshwater invertebrates, accompanied by newts, frogs and toads. Swimmers were sometimes surprised to find themselves sharing the moat with a grass snake that had forsaken its field-edge habitat to hunt for amphibian prey.

*

ABOVE LEFT
Pumping out the water into the adjoining dry moat.

ABOVE RIGHT
Moat dredging team of two, plus one large excavator.

LIFE AT WALNUT TREE FARM

The leaf- and stick-laden spoil spread out next to the moat after dredging. When it was dry enough, it was levelled off by tractor and zig-zag harrow.

BELOW
The spring feed returned water levels in the moat to normal within a few days.

New life returns to the moat,
spring 2017.

The hut's cousin, the railway wagon in the adjoining field, was also showing signs of disrepair: a few of its boards had worked themselves loose and it had grown a thick layer of lichen. Having been designed for thousands of miles of heavy haulage, the double-layered hardwood boards and steel brackets were basically still good. However, gravity had taken a strong grip on the frame, which was slowly rotating and causing the brick piles that supported its two-ton weight to lean at a worrying angle. This gentle pirouette followed by the inevitable crash was likely to destroy the entire wagon, so we jammed wooden props in place, some of them up against a half-sunken hayturner. This 'temporary' measure held disaster at bay for nearly ten years. Then, in 2016, we persuaded a neighbour – who happened to have some heavy lifting machinery on hire – to lift the wagon off its insubstantial legs and place it on the ground while a replacement stand of six concrete-filled half oil-drums were set in position. The hours it took to do this overran the hire time for the heavy-lifting machinery, so we called up a smaller but similar contraption from an obliging farmer neighbour. This machine strained every sinew to lift the bulky box into position. Catastrophe seemed near as its back wheels rose off the ground and warning lights flashed – but, eventually, the job was done and could be crossed off the list.

*

OPPOSITE
The railway wagon on its new
half-barrel legs.

LIFE AT WALNUT TREE FARM

ABOVE LEFT
The shackle and bolt on the
door of the railway wagon.

ABOVE RIGHT
The wagon's heavy sliding
door, facing south onto the
meadow.

RIGHT
'Slow but sure combustion':
the Tortoise brand wood-
burner in the railway wagon.

ABOVE
Inside the wagon, wood-
burner and Moroccan lamps.

LEFT
Built to last millions of rail
miles...

201

LIFE AT WALNUT TREE FARM

At just twelve acres, the farm is not large enough to return a monetary income of any size through crops or livestock. The longstanding arrangement with the cattle farmer on the other side of the common – to cut and take the hay every summer – boosted the diversity of the meadow flowers growing at Walnut Tree Farm rather than its owner's wallet. To survive and hold their own against thuggish grasses, wildflowers need soil that is low in nutrients, and the annual cutting and removal of the hay made sure this was the case. Unfortunately, once the Mellis Common cattle herd was reduced in size in 2012, the hay from the farm's meadows was no longer wanted. That summer a tractor and flail blitzed the hay down to rot back into the soil. It was safe to cut it like this for a year or two, but if this practice continued over a longer period, the meadow would soon have been invaded by a rank growth of thistle, plantain and ragwort. It's difficult to find another farm to take the hay. No pesticide, herbicide or chemical fertilizer has touched the meadows for more than forty years. On our lean soil the grasses – the most nutritious component for livestock – do not grow in such vigour and abundance as they do in more monocultural meadows.

To keep the ragwort at bay, we pull up by hand any specimens we find, roots and all, and toss them onto the bonfire. Even before the bright yellow florets open, the blueish tinge of their leaves can be detected from several feet away. The evidence as to whether ragwort is actually harmful to horses and livestock is

OPPOSITE
A recently cut meadow dries
out before hay-baling.

Sunset over Mellis Common.
Hall Farm, the nearest
neighbouring farm, can be
seen in the distance.

Hay bales on the common.

A Ferguson TED20 (or Grey Fergie) tractor on the middle field.

inconclusive, but its presence in a meadow will knock a hay deal dead on the spot.

The farm's main crop derives from its mile of hedge and small wood. Fuel for fireplace and wood-burner is dragged from the hedgerows. A dead tree felled by a strong gale provides a large quantity of wood, as did the undergrowth cleared to gain access to the moat for digging. Only the thinnest brash is burnt on the bonfire or chipped: any stick over an inch or so thick is good for the fireplace. There must be a saying about the wisdom of gathering firewood when you can, along the lines of the old saying about fixing the roof when the sun is shining. If such a maxim exists, it's not followed strictly enough at Walnut Tree Farm (which relies

LIFE AT WALNUT TREE FARM

Using chains, the tractor
pulls dead elm from the
hedgerows for firewood.

TOP LEFT AND CENTRE
Massive logs reveal the
recent attentions of a
splitting axe.

ABOVE AND LEFT
Three glimpses of the
1960s Moto Guzzi Ercole
motocarro ('motorbike-
truck'): excellent for
transporting sawn logs
from field to woodshed.

209

on the same heating system as it did in the sixteenth century). Wood-cutting and gathering is tough but enjoyable work. Having put on suitable protective clothing, all you need is a bramble slasher, a splitting axe, a sharp and well-tuned chainsaw (which runs on two-stroke oil) and a chipper to reduce the mountain of brash into a small pile of chips; a tractor (our old machine has two tanks and requires two different types of fuel) and three-wheel tipper truck for transportation; and a dry woodshed in which to store the precious commodity. By late spring the woodsheds are usually empty, and any logs left out in the open are too damp to burn. A cold spell in April or early May sends us rummaging into the farm's various sheds for worm-eaten furniture, pallets or old doors – anything wooden that can be burnt to give off precious heat.

Over our first few years of living at Walnut Tree Farm, we found that most of the jobs that needed doing around the place entailed an unspoken dialogue with Roger. Whether it was repairing the tractor or another item of farm machinery, or gathering fire-wood from a recently fallen tree, or mending the roof or repairing a window – we realized, sooner or later, that the knowledge of 'how to do it' already resided within us.

Slowly but surely, hand over hand, a process of transferral from Roger to us was taking place.

OPPOSITE
The Moto Guzzi seen front on: load capacity of near a ton, hydraulic tipping back, five forward gears and reverse. Sophisticated and robust engineering make for a vehicle that is both reliable and reasonably simple to repair.

CHAPTER 7

Living, cooking, walking, watching

Snow, early morning. Settled on everything.
Trees sugared and frosted.
Tracks (a few pheasants and a feral cat) in the snow.

NOTES FROM WALNUT TREE FARM,
'DECEMBER'

COME LATE AUTUMN AT THE FARM, YOU CAN'T deny the fact much longer: it will soon be winter and, as the weather gets colder, thicker and thicker layers of clothing will be required. During the winter months (and parts of the autumn and spring), a house without central heating requires barrowloads of dry wood to raise the temperature inside to something approaching comfortable. Total warmth is not possible. The warm areas of the house are very localized: in front of the Aga; around (but not too far from) the central fireplace; and in bed. Everywhere else is simply cold. Guests at the farm, most of whom are of course used to central heating, often keep their coats on indoors. As places of maximum physical comfort, the Aga and fireplace are the focal points of the house. Aga stoves have become symbols of rural affluence, and as such their presence in non-rural contexts smacks of middle-class affectation. But the Aga at Walnut Tree Farm, installed in 1973, is an essential, practical feature of the house. In addition to cooking food, its functions include heating the kitchen and drying clothes. The longevity of Agas is legendary, and they are easy to service and repair (a task which, in this case, is carried out by the owner).

You can't grill in the Aga. Meat and vegetables done over the open fire, with toasted bread on the side, are delicious. Perhaps this method of cooking is an expression of a primeval urge – a desire to prepare food as our ancestors did. An iron hook sticking out of the

PREVIOUS SPREAD
Walnut Tree Farm, winter 2017: the tracks in the snow are those of a wheelbarrow, used to ferry the precious fuel to the fireplace.

OPPOSITE
The central hearth of the living room. A weathered stick, found by Roger in the Rhinog Mountains of North Wales, hangs on the bressumer beam above the inglenook fireplace. The 'witching' marks on the beam were scratched by previous residents of the farm, long before Roger moved in.

LIFE AT WALNUT TREE FARM

LIVING, COOKING, WALKING, WATCHING

LIFE AT WALNUT TREE FARM

brickwork seven feet up the chimney is evidence that the occupants of Walnut Tree Farm cooked in this way 450 years ago. More often than not we cook at least part of our winter evening meal over a fire of ash, oak or elm. The smoke drifting up the chimney and across the fields carries aromas that would be familiar in those parts of the world where this age-old type of cooking remains the norm.

After a few years of grilling we began to worry about the condition of the chimney flue. Given the regularity of our winter meat-grilling over the open fire, surely the grease must be building up to levels normally associated with the extractor ducting of a well-patronized kebab joint. One spark would be all that was needed to set the chimney ablaze! But the prospect of calling a chimney sweep and the inevitable eyeball-rolling when the unpleasant nature of the task became apparent, was too much to bear. So, once our anxiety about the fire risk had reached a high enough level to initiate action, I donned overalls, gloves and dust mask. The fireplace is eight feet wide and three feet deep at the base, and I was able to use a long ladder to ascend the tapering chimney shaft and half wedge myself at roofline level. Working my way slowly downwards, to avoid having grit fall in my eyes, I proceeded to scrape and brush the crusty black brickwork. As I did so, I was surprised to find little trace of the thick layer of sooty grease I had expected. With the surface of the chimney flue restored to a safe condition, it was on with the winter mixed grill!

OPPOSITE TOP LEFT
Away from the fire, the ambient winter room temperature rarely rises above 10 degrees Celsius.

OPPOSITE CENTRE LEFT
Locally made merguez sausages, grilling over glowing embers.

OPPOSITE RIGHT
A long way from the Mediterranean... but Suffolk merguez taste nearly as good as the Maghrebi originals when cooked on an open fire.

Looking up the chimney flue: eight feet by three feet at the base, and tapering to nine inches by twelve inches at the top. Highly flammable soot has to be swept regularly.

Brickwork scarred and
patched from nearly 500
years of use.

The room downstairs at the
north end of the house is
now a bedroom, after years
of use as a study.

ABOVE LEFT
The hand-worn front door,
with latches old and modern.

ABOVE RIGHT
Revamped outside WC,
with salvaged stained-glass
window.

RIGHT
Walnut Tree Farm was once
known as Rose Cottages. Forty
rose bushes still grow close to
the house, generating enough
petals to make rose water.

LEFT
Hedgerow elixirs: apply labels
or forget contents.

ABOVE
The farm seen from the door
of the shepherd's hut.

ABOVE LEFT
A common spotted orchid amongst the buttercups and grasses.

ABOVE RIGHT
A pyramid orchid.

RIGHT
Tufted vetch flowers on into late summer.

OPPOSITE
Orchids taken from the hay cut.

Like the house, the repaired shepherd's hut contains primeval elements and lighting the hut's small but perfectly adequate wood-burner takes a certain knack. When things go smoothly, the successful passing of the flame from match to paper to twigs to chunks of wood, culminating with a strong roar as the air is drawn in and the fire really gets going, is a joy. But the fire-lighting process is not always wrinkle-free. Sometimes the flame flickers and falters, producing a back-draught of reeking smoke. The required puffing into the dying embers as you try to salvage a botched attempt can make your head spin. This uncertainty of outcome makes for a harmless form of gambling, and when things work out the win is especially satisfying.

Inside the hut, you feel a close proximity to weather and wild beasts, but no threat from either. When a bird alights on the tin roof, you can guess the species quite accurately from the noise its talons make and from the timbre of its call. A loud and heavy scrape, followed by continued scratchings and rustlings after landing, almost certainly indicates the arrival of a barn owl. Pigeons always flap their wings noisily as they depart, but barn owls leave soundlessly. So, if the scrapings on the tin roof of the hut cease suddenly, with no accompanying flutter, you can be pretty sure that an owl has launched itself silently into the night. The hut's old, lumpy horse-hair mattress provides a surprisingly good night's sleep.

*

ABOVE LEFT
The meadow at summer's
end, glimpsed through
the open window of the
shepherd's hut.

ABOVE RIGHT
The tarred roof of the
hut, with the tree line of
Cowpasture Lane beyond.

ABOVE
The hut seen through
bunches of ash keys in
late summer.

LEFT
Inside the shepherd's hut:
a luxurious berth on an ocean
of grass.

231

ABOVE LEFT
Getting the wood-burner in
the shepherd's hut going for
the first time, autumn 2018.

ABOVE RIGHT
Shadows thrown by the
Moroccan lamp.

ABOVE AND RIGHT
Summer dawn.

OPPOSITE
Winter dawn.

234

Looking at photographs of Walnut Tree Farm from the early 1970s, one is immediately struck by the smaller size of the trees and hedges. In comparison with today's luxuriant growth, the landscape seems almost bare. Now, with a considerably weightier biomass encircling the farm, there is almost a feeling of being closed in, especially on warm, still days in summer. Autumn and winter, however, restore openness to the surroundings of the farm, allowing forgotten views and the structures of trees and hedges to reappear. Seasonal gales blow the freshly fallen leaves in all directions, causing them to gather in dips, ditches and hollows, which fill with drifts of copper-brown and livid yellow.

Over the last decade, based on casual observation, previously scarce wildlife seems to be appearing more frequently around the farm. Buzzards are ranging further from their stronghold in Thornham: in 2018 a pair nested in the triangular wood planted in 1986 by Roger and Serena in the corner of the railway field. If you walk the fields on summer nights – best done without a torch – you may well catch the glimmer of *Lampyris noctiluca*, the common glow-worm. One year, after the hay cut, a particular field was dotted with dozens of their fluorescent green thoraxes, like runway lights on an airfield, the glow of the wingless females guiding the airborne males in to mate. Alongside these bioluminescent residents, the farm is home to an ever-growing population of hares, kingfishers, owls, woodpeckers, snakes and crested newts.

OPPOSITE
The little wood in the corner of the railway field, autumn 2018.

Scenes from the long hot summer of 2018: (top row) wild hops, fungus, black poplar bark with lichen and grass snake; (bottom row) blackthorn bushes (with a decent crop of sloes), wren's nest and glow-worm.

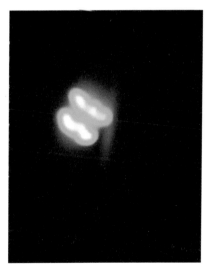

Summer 2018, cart pond
by shepherd's hut.

LIFE AT WALNUT TREE FARM

Ash bower, 2018.

It is not only the farm that has increased its imprint on the landscape. Since it was levelled in 1981, Cowpasture Lane has enjoyed a resurgence in growth under its protected status. I walk its quarter of a mile nearly every day, all year round, usually in the evening accompanied by our dog, Hercle. For a large part of the year, my walk takes place outside of daylight hours, but not necessarily in total darkness. A strong moon, especially shining on snow, floods the lane with blue-grey light. Only a week or two later, however, low cloud and a different phase of the moon might well reduce visibility to next to nothing. But I still don't need a torch: the familiar gentle undulations and occasional speck of light from a house a mile away, glimpsed through the trees, keep my course clear of the bramble and blackthorn on either side of the lane.

Whether undertaken by day or night, the pleasure of this daily walk along Cowpasture Lane never palls. The variations of season, weather and hour of day make for an inexhaustible kaleidoscope of views. The arrow-straight railway line cutting across the lane where the farm's fields end doesn't diminish its attractions for me. The trains flash by in a few seconds and, in the calm that follows, it is the notion of one thousand years of slow travel by foot or hoof that pervades the senses, not the roar of multiple tons of steel travelling at over 100mph. Walkers who follow the lane towards Thornham from Mellis Common between late spring and mid-autumn are hedged in by dense growth. The trees and bushes rise up and meet

OPPOSITE
The husk of the clinker-built dinghy.

The entrance to Cowpasture
Lane on Mellis Common.

Cowpasture Lane in autumn.

LIFE AT WALNUT TREE FARM

ABOVE LEFT
The line of Cowpasture Lane,
seen from the field that
almost swallowed it up.

ABOVE RIGHT
The lane in winter.

RIGHT
The London-to-Norwich main
line under sunny skies.

The 600-yard stretch of Cowpasture Lane beyond the railway line was deprived of its hedgerow in 1970.

overhead, creating a tunnel that blocks off all but the briefest views of the farm to the left or the expanse of field to the right.

As the leaves turn from myriad shades of green to soft yellows, reds and browns, and then start to fall from the trees, various components of the farm are revealed across the meadows. First you might notice the crumbling side boards and ivy-clad spokes of the bullock cart, defying gravity for a few more years before its unavoidable collapse. A few yards on, the railway wagon, barn and woodshed come into view, with the gable end of the house just visible behind. Walk a little further, and you will be rewarded by the south-facing glow of terracotta pantiles, three dormer windows and the chimney. Listen carefully and you might hear a splash, followed by a cry of anguish from a swimmer taking an icy plunge. Beyond a thick hedge that runs off the lane at right angles, you will encounter another meadow, bordered by the same hedge and punctuated by the skeletons of elm trees that died young, as elm trees do. They have stood here for years, barkless and sun-bleached. Squint and you might just see the straight parallel lines of a man-made structure between lane and house. The curved tin roof and weatherboarded sides of the shepherd's hut poke out from behind a stand of blackthorn encroaching on the field. On cold days, thin strands of smoke from the hut's wood-burner drift across the lane on a north-westerly breeze. A hundred yards further on, another much thicker hedge cuts to the left. It has a ditch running down its

Tall oat-grass on the missing
section of the lane.

centre, which, when dry, forms another semi-subterranean pathway between the fields. The next and last field before the London–Norwich railway line holds no sheds, wagons or discarded farm implements. The hornbeam, ash and oak wood planted on its far side in the late 1980s is now tall and dense enough to shade out all but a few light-shy plants on the leaf-litter floor. Beyond the line, on the bare section of lane, the wide-open space has some appeal for skylarks. All year round they inhabit the thin strip of vegetation bordering the path, holding tight to stalks of false oat-grass. They fling themselves into the air when you are only a pace or two away from them, singing their way up and out of sight.

The farm's biodiversity list includes another, more controversial, species, whose forebears can be seen in the building-site images from 1971 lapping up saucers of milk. A population of feral cats continues to eke out an existence in abandoned cars and sheds. We hope they are sticking to a diet of rabbits or pheasant – and have not developed a taste for kingfisher! The tribe's days, however, are numbered. About ten years ago a local cat protection society was alerted to the proliferation of wild felines in the area. They trapped the cats, sterilized them, then released them back into the wild. Roger's beloved black cat Alphonse was among those nabbed in the round-up. He bore a snipped ear as a mark of the loss of his manhood until the end of his days. Sightings of gang members are now increasingly rare.

One of the last feral
cats keeps a wary eye on
proceedings.

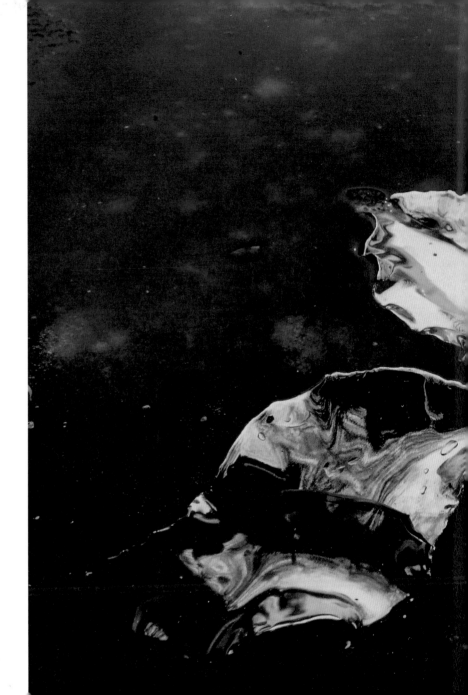

Jasmin's land art installation.
Porcelain and gold lustre
leaves on the melting ice of
the moat, winter 2018.